Mrs. H. Robinson
214, Colonial Dr.
Thomasville, N.C.

THE
INSPIRED LETTERS
In Clearest English

Prepared by

FRANK C. LAUBACH, Ph.D.

THOMAS NELSON & SONS

TORONTO   NEW YORK   EDINBURGH

First Printing, March, 1956
Second Printing, October, 1956

Library of Congress Catalogue Card Number: 56-7958

TABLE OF CONTENTS

TO THE READER

This is far and away the clearest English version of the New Testament Letters. The need for such a clear version has been felt by millions of people. The four Gospels and the Acts are easy to read. But when people try Paul's "Letter to the Romans" most of them are soon lost in involved sentences and the difficult argument of a profound scholar. Many people, after reading a few paragraphs, give up the Letters altogether, saying: "I can't make sense out of this." Yet if these Letters are rewritten in familiar language, they tell a marvelous story. They are the most priceless good news for all of us that God ever sent to this earth. Most of the Letters were written many years before any of the Gospels appeared, so these Letters are the first information we have about Jesus. They reveal what Christians thought about Christ some twenty years after His resurrection. Here we find the churches tingling with the glory of the risen Christ, and strong with the power of the Holy Spirit.

To help the truth in these letters to stand forth clear and easy enough even for a child to understand, it was necessary to follow three principles:

(1) Sometimes a word had to be added, sometimes a short phrase, sometimes even a sentence, to help us understand. When Paul wrote to his Christian friends, they knew exactly what he meant, and sometimes his letters stung them until they wept. But the ordinary person of today studying Paul's letter to the Christians in Rome rubs his head and says, "What in the world is this all about?" If people weep today over these letters, it is only with despair because they cannot understand them. By adding brief explanatory phrases, these letters can all be made clear. A book is not really "translated" into *our* language until *we know what it means*.

(2) If we are to be crystal clear, we must give up trying to pre-
serve the style, or word order, or sentence structure of the
original Greek. For example, the very first sentence in Romans
is one hundred words long. English translations usually try to
save that long sentence; but in the translation you have in your
hands, you will find that it has been cut into sixteen short simple
sentences. (You might want to look at them—page 13.) But the
meaning is just as accurately preserved in this book as it is in
any other translation.

(3) Every difficult word has been changed into a well-known
word, or into a short phrase. *Almost* every word in this book
(excepting names of people and places) is among the two thousand most frequently used words in the English language. You
will not find any hard words like "gospel," "redemption," "right-
eousness," "justification," "futility," or "covenant." You will find
these words replaced with easy words like "good news," "bought
on the cross," "made right with God," "made just in God's
sight," "death and decay," and "agreement"—these are all well-
known English words.

This volume is *Number Four* in a graded series of books aimed
at teaching people to read the Bible. A Graded Series like this
is being written in over fifty other languages around the world.

Here is the Graded Series in English:

1st Book ... *Streamlined English* with the Teacher's Manual
—a reading readiness book for those who cannot read English.
(Published by the Macmillan Company.)

2nd Book ... *The Story of Jesus,* in ninety chapters, to prepare the reader to read the Four Gospels.

3rd Book ... The Four Gospels and Acts in the Revised
Standard Version. (Published by Thomas Nelson and Sons.)

4th Book ... This volume in your hands—*The Inspired
Letters*.

5th Book ... The Letters of the New Testament in the Revised
Standard Version.

6th Book . . . The Book of Revelation and the Old Testament in the Revised Standard Version.

So this book in your hand is a preparation for the Revised Standard Version; it is not a *substitute* for reading the Bible.

Mimeographed copies of the manuscript were sent to sixty of the leading New Testament scholars of the United States and England. This resulted in hundreds of improvements. We are greatly indebted to all who carefully examined and criticized the manuscript. I wish to express special appreciation to Dr. Eugene Nida and his associates for the many constructive suggestions designed to make the translation more closely reflective of the meaning of the Greek text. The letters of Paul and Peter and Jude and the Letter to the Hebrews are difficult in all translations, and especially so in the languages of Asia and North Africa. They are far more difficult to read than the Gospels and Acts. Some day they must all be made simpler.

While many scholars and others have offered their suggestions to this book, none of them is responsible for the version as it now appears, excepting myself. The one and only excuse I have for offering this simplification is that I have had twenty-five years of experience in making books clear to illiterates and new literates in over two hundred languages. I have the profoundest admiration for the great Biblical scholars, and I shall be happy if I have helped to make the results of their deep learning and lifetime toil available for the three fourths of our world who want the thoughts of the scientists and scholars spelled out in easy words.

I want also to thank many other people who helped me in typing and retyping and reretyping this text; many did it as a labor of love. Twenty of the devoted people at Koinonia read the text in pairs, along with the ten best-known copyrighted translations, to make sure that I had not unintentionally plagiarized.

FRANK C. LAUBACH

THE INSPIRED LETTERS

PAUL'S LETTER
TO THE CHRISTIANS IN ROME

From: *Paul*   From Corinth, Greece

To: *The Christians in Rome*

1 I, Paul, am a servant of Jesus Christ. He called me to be His apostle. He selected me to tell the Good News of God. ² Long ago God promised this Good News in the holy writings of His prophets. ³ It is the Good News about His Son Jesus. Jesus came as a man through the family of David. ⁴ He was declared the Son of God, He had the power of the Holy Spirit. This was made plain when He rose from the dead. Our Lord Jesus Christ ⁵ treated me with great favor. He made me His apostle to all the Gentiles. In His name I am bringing them to believe and obey. ⁶ This includes you. You, too, are called to belong to Jesus Christ. ⁷ I am writing to all those in Rome whom God loves. God has called you to be His people.

God's grace be with you. May you have peace from God our Father and from the Lord Jesus Christ.

⁸ I keep thanking God for all of you. I thank him through Jesus Christ. The news of your faith is told all over the world. ⁹ With all my heart I am serving God as I tell people the Good News of His Son. And God is my witness that I never stop remembering you when I pray. ¹⁰ I keep asking God that I may at last succeed in coming to visit you, if God is willing. ¹¹ I long to see you. I want to pass on to you some gift of the spirit to make you strong. ¹² I want to be encouraged by your faith. And I want you to be encouraged by my faith. ¹³ Brothers, I want you to know that I have often planned to come to you. Up to

13

now I have been prevented from coming. I hope to gather a harvest among you as well as among the rest of the nations. [14] I owe a debt to Greeks and to all other nations. I owe a debt to the wise and to those with no education. [15] That is why I long to preach the Good News to you also in Rome.

[16] I never feel ashamed of the Good News. It is God's power to save everybody who has faith. It can save the Jew, and it can also save the Greek. [17] God is good. We who have faith see how good He is to all who put their faith in Him. It is written:

"Every man who has faith is counted just by God
and so shall live."

[18] But the anger of God is appearing from heaven against all evil men who break God's law. They fight the truth by their evil deeds. [19] What can be known about God is plain. God has shown it to them. [20] Although God cannot be seen, His nature can be understood in the things He has made. Ever since the world began the everlasting power of God could be seen. So they have no excuse for their sins. [21] They knew God, but they did not honor Him or thank Him as God. Their minds were dark. Their thoughts made no sense. [22] They claimed to be wise but were fools. [23] They did not worship the everliving God who made them. Instead they chose to worship objects which they made to look like men or birds or animals or serpents. [24] For this reason God gave their hearts up to evil sex desires. It is a shame what they did with their bodies between themselves. [25] They exchanged the truth about God for a lie. [26] God let them become slaves of every low passion. Their women exchanged natural relations for those against nature. [27] Men also gave up natural relations with women and burned with passion for one another. They were doing disgusting things with other men. And they received in their own persons the punishment due them for doing wrong.

[28] Since they did not see fit to recognize God, He gave them up to low thoughts and bad habits. [29] They were filled with all

kinds of sin and evil desires. They hated others and coveted what they possessed. They fought and murdered. They were false, they burned with ill will. They talked against people and [30] destroyed their good name. They hated God. They were vain and proud. They were always boasting and looking down on others. They were always planning some evil. They did not obey their parents. [31] They were foolish, they could not be trusted, they were hard-hearted and without pity. [32] They knew God's law. They knew that those who do such things deserve to die. Yet they did these things and praised others who did them.

2 You have no excuse, O man, whoever you are, when you judge any one else. When you pass judgment on him you sentence yourself. For you are doing the very things you judge wrong. [2] We know it is right for the judgment of God to fall on those who do such things. [3] If you do what you judge evil in others, do you think that you will escape the judgment of God? [4] Or are you trying to take advantage of God's kindness and patience and long suffering? Do you not see that God is kind in order to lead you to turn from sin? [5] But because your heart is hard and you refuse to turn from your sin, you are storing up the anger of God against you. His anger will be plain on the day when He passes His just sentence upon you. [6] He will reward every man according to his works. [7] Those who are patient in doing good and who seek for glory and honor and everlasting life will be given life eternal. [8] But those who quarrel and do not obey the truth but obey evil will be punished by an angry God. [9] There will be suffering and trouble for every man who does evil, for the Jew and also for the Greek. [10] But there will be glory and honor and peace for every one who does good, for the Jew and also for the Greek. [11] God does not favor one race above another.

[12] All who sin outside the law of Moses will be destroyed outside the law. All who accept the law of Moses and sin under it will be judged by that law. [13] Hearing the law is not enough

15

alone to make a man right with God. Only those who obey the law will be counted just in God's sight. [14] The Gentiles do not have the law of Moses. When they do by nature what the law requires, they have their own law. [15] They show that what the law requires is written in their hearts. Their sense of right and wrong guides them. Their minds, full of doubts, will [16] condemn them or perhaps excuse them on the day when God judges them. My Good News is that God will judge the secret lives of all men, by Jesus Christ.

[17] You who call yourself a Jew put your hope in the law of Moses. You boast about your relation to God. [18] You say you know His will and can tell what is right because you know the law. [19] You are sure you are a guide to the blind and a light to those in the dark. [20] You think you can train the foolish and teach the young. You think you have the knowledge and truth which is in the law of Moses. [21] Why, then, is it, that you teach others but do not teach yourself? You preach that a man must not steal. Do you steal? [22] You say a man must not commit adultery. Do you commit adultery? You hate idols. Do you steal from temples? [23] You pride yourself in the law. Yet do you break the law and show no respect for God? [24] "Because you do this, the name of God is cursed among the Gentiles," as God's Word says.

[25] It is a help to be circumcised only if you obey the law. But if you break the law you might as well not be circumcised. [26] Suppose a man who is not circumcised keeps the commands of the law. Do you not think he will be counted circumcised? [27] Some people who are not circumcised do keep the law; then they show how evil you Jews are. For you are circumcised, you know the law, and yet you break it. [28] He is not a real Jew who is a Jew only on the outside. It is not enough for the flesh of a man to be circumcised. [29] A real Jew must be a Jew inside; his heart must be circumcised. He must be circumcised in spirit, not just in the letter of the law. For his praise ought to come, not from men, but from God.

3 What advantage then has the Jew? What is the good of being circumcised? ² There is much good in every way. First of all, the Jews were trusted with the promises of God. ³ Some Jews were not faithful. But if they were not faithful, did that keep God from being faithful? ⁴ Of course not. God must be true to His promise even though every man is false. Our Holy Book says to God:

> "When you are judged
> you will prove that you are true.
> You will win the victory."

⁵ Our evil lives only serve to show the justice of God. If that is true, can we say that God is doing wrong to punish us? (Some men actually do talk like this.) ⁶ Of course God is not doing wrong. How could God judge the world any other way? ⁷ My being false helps make it more clear that God is true. Why, then, some men ask, am I condemned for sinning? ⁸ Why not do evil if good comes out of it? (Some people make a false charge that this is what I teach. I never taught that, but if I did I should deserve their blame.)

⁹ Am I saying that we Jews are better off than other people? Oh no! I have already said that Jews and Greeks were all alike. They are all under the power of sin, ¹⁰ just as God's Word says:

> "None is really good, no, not even one.
> ¹¹ No one understands God. No one seeks Him.
> ¹² All have turned away. They have all done wrong.
> No one does right, not even one.
> ¹³ Their throats are like open graves.
> They use their tongue to trick people.
> Snakes' poison is under their lips.
> ¹⁴ Their mouth is full of curses and bitter words.
> ¹⁵ Their feet are swift to make blood flow.
> ¹⁶ In their paths are ruin and pain.
> ¹⁷ The way of peace they do not know.
> ¹⁸ They do not have the fear of God before their eyes."

[19] We know therefore that all who were under the law of Moses have sinned. So the law has spoken its sentence against them. So every mouth is stopped. The whole world is held to account before God. [20] No human being was ever just in God's sight by obeying the law, because every one has broken the law. The law has only helped men to see their sin.

[21] But now we see how good God is! He saves us in another way outside the law of Moses. The law and prophets bear witness to this other way. [22] It is this: Every person who has faith in Jesus Christ is forgiven and made right with God. For God makes no difference between people. [23] They have all sinned. They all fall short of the glory of God. [24] But God shows His forgiving love toward them and considers them just. In order to do this, He made them a free gift. That free gift was Jesus Christ. He gave His life to pay the price of their sin. [25] God offered up Christ to wipe out our sin with His blood. We can receive God's gift simply with faith. Thus we see how good God is. He is so patient that He forgives all our past sins. [26] He counts us just, if we have faith in Jesus. That is how just and kind He is!

[27] What then becomes of our pride in being Jews? It all has to go. Are we saved because our works are good? No! We must depend on our faith, not on the law, to become right with God. [28] I say that God clears a man of his sin, not because the man obeys the law, but only because the man has faith in Christ. [29] Is God the God of the Jews only? No indeed, He is the God of the Gentiles too. [30] For He is one God, not many. He will clear the circumcised Jews if they have faith. And He will clear the Gentiles who are not circumcised if they have faith. [31] Do we then throw out the law when we depend on faith? Certainly not. We hold to it as the law of God.

4 What shall we say about our father Abraham? Why was he right with God? [2] Abraham was a just man and did good works. He had something he could be proud of before men. But it was

not his good works that made him just before God. It was his faith. ³ For what does God's Word say?

> "Abraham had faith in God
> that is why God counted him just."

⁴ If a man works, his wages are not a gift. They are a debt owed to him. ⁵ But no work that a man can do makes him just before God. A man must trust in the gift of God's kindness to forgive his sins. It is a man's faith which makes him right with God. ⁶ David told us that a man is blessed if God counts him just without considering his works. David says:

> ⁷ "Blessed are those whose evil deeds are forgiven.
> Blessed are those whose sins are covered.
> ⁸ Blessed is a man if God does not count his sin
> against him."

⁹ Let us ask again? Is this blessed gift only for those who are circumcised? Or is it given also to those who are not circumcised? It is given to both. I told you that on account of his faith Abraham was counted a just man. ¹⁰ When was he counted just? Was it before he was circumcised or after? It was before he was circumcised, it was not after. ¹¹ He was not circumcised until after his faith had been counted to make him right with God. He was later circumcised as a sign or a seal that he had been made right with God. God's purpose was to make Abraham the father of all who are not circumcised, but who have faith, and so are counted right with God. ¹² Of course Abraham is also the father of the circumcised if they follow Abraham's example. That is to say, they too must have faith such as Abraham had before he was circumcised.

¹³ God's promise came to Abraham and to his children that they should some day be given the earth. This promise did not come through the law of Moses. It came through Abraham's faith, which made him right with God. ¹⁴ If it were true that only those who keep the law of Moses were to be given the earth, then faith would be of no use. God's promise to Abraham would

mean nothing. But in fact the law saves nobody. [15] All the law can do is to bring the anger of God upon those who break it. (But where there is no law to break, nobody can break it.)

[16] This then is why we depend upon faith. The promise of God rests upon His forgiving love. His promise is sure for all His children who have faith. He promises it, not only to those who live by the law, but also to all others who share the kind of faith Abraham had. Abraham is the father of everybody who has faith.

[17] It is written that God told Abraham: "I will make you the father of many nations." Abraham had faith that God would keep that promise. He believed that God could make the dead live again. He believed that God would create things which did not then exist. [18] So Abraham believed that he would indeed become the father of many nations. He had been told: "Your children shall become many nations." He kept on believing this even when all hope seemed to be gone. [19] His faith did not grow weak even when his body was nearly dead (for he was about a hundred years old). His faith did not grow weak although Sarah was far too old to have children. [20] He did not doubt that God would keep His promise. His faith grew stronger as he kept on giving glory to God. [21] He was sure that God was able to do what He had promised. [22] It was because Abraham had such faith that he was counted just. [23] Those words in Genesis which said, "Abraham's faith was counted to his credit," were not written for his sake alone. [24] They were written for our sakes also. Our faith will be counted to our credit too, if we have faith in God who raised Jesus our Lord from the dead. [25] We must believe that Jesus was put to death for our sins and that He was raised to make us right with God.

5 We are made right with God by our faith. Therefore we have peace with God through our Lord Jesus Christ. [2] Through Christ we have been admitted to this forgiving love on which we now stand. We sing with joy in our hope of sharing God's glory.

[3] Even when we suffer we sing with joy. We know how suffering makes us patient. [4] Then patience produces firm character. Then character produces hope. [5] Our hope will never leave us, because God's love has been poured into our hearts by the Holy Spirit which He has given us.

[6] While we could not help ourselves, at the right time Christ died for us evil men. [7] No one wants to die even for a just man, although perhaps for a good man some one might dare to die. [8] But even when we were in sin, Christ died for us. That is how God showed His love for us. [9] We are now right with God through the blood of Christ. And Christ will save us from God's anger. [10] We were enemies of God, but the death of His son makes us friends of God. Now that we have become His friends, we shall be saved by the living Christ. [11] With joy we praise God because our Lord Jesus Christ has made us friends of God once more.

[12] Sin came into the world through one man, Adam, and death came because Adam sinned. Then death spread to all other men, because all men sinned. [13] Long before the law of Moses was given, sin was in the world. But sin is not counted as law-breaking where there is no law. [14] Yet sin brought death and death ruled from Adam to Moses. Death ruled over everybody, even those who did not sin as Adam had sinned.

The man Adam was from one point of view a type of the One Man, Christ, Who was to come. [15] I do not mean to say that God's free gift was like Adam's sin. It was just the opposite. After the one man, Adam, broke God's law, many died. Then God in His grace gave us that other Man, Christ, as a free gift. Christ did enough and more than enough to make men live. [16] So God's free gift and Adam's sin had exactly opposite effects. After Adam sinned God's judgment was that he deserved death. But God's free gift sets us free from our many sins and makes us right with God once more. [17] That one man, Adam, when he sinned, put all men under the rule of death. But that other Man, Jesus Christ, makes men right with God so that they shall live and rule like kings. This He does for all who accept God's rich forgiving love and His free gift.

[18] Well, then! One man's sin led all men to be sentenced to death. The other Man's right act sets all men free and gives them life. [19] One man, Adam, broke God's law and so he made many men sin. The other Man, Christ, obeyed God's will and so He made many men right with God.

[20] The law of Moses came so that men could see how many of God's laws they were breaking. Their sense of sin increased, but God's grace was always more than enough to forgive them. [21] Once sin ruled and death ruled with it. But now the grace of God rules. And through Jesus Christ men can all become right with God and have everlasting life.

6 Shall we then continue to sin in order that there may be more grace? Can we say that? [2] Certainly not! We died to sin. Therefore, how can we go on living in sin? [3] Don't you realize that all of us who have been baptized into Christ Jesus were baptized into His death? [4] In our baptism we died and were buried with Him. And just as He was raised from the dead through the Father's glory, we too are to live a new kind of life like His.

[5] We have been united with Him by dying as He died. That is why we are sure to be united with Him by rising from the dead as He rose. [6] Our old self was nailed to the cross with Him, to put our old sinning body to death. Now we are no longer slaves to sin. [7] Any one who has died is freed from sin. [8] So then, if we have died with Christ, we believe that we shall also live with Christ. [9] Christ has been raised from the dead and will never die again. Death has lost all its power over Him. [10] When He died He was once and for all dead to sin. The life He lives He lives to God. [11] Because you are united to Christ Jesus you must consider yourselves also dead to the call of sin and alive to the call of God.

[12] So do not let sin rule your bodies, which are going to die.

Do not let sin make you obey the body's passions. ¹³ Do not yield to sin with any part of your body to make it a tool of evil. You have been brought from death to life, so yield yourselves to God. Yield all parts of your body to God, as tools of what is right. ¹⁴ Sin must have no power over you. You are not under the law of Moses, but you are under the grace of God.

¹⁵ What does that mean? Are we allowed to sin because we are not under law but under God's grace! Certainly not! ¹⁶ Do you not see that if you yield yourselves to any one you are his slaves? Either you are slaves to sin, which leads to death, or you obey God, which leads to the good life. ¹⁷ I thank God that though you were once slaves of sin, yet now you obey from your hearts the higher way of living. This is the higher standard which we taught you to obey. ¹⁸ That is how you have been set free from sin, and have become slaves only of what is right. ¹⁹ I must use very common words because your weak natures need plain talk. You once yielded parts of your body to sex vice and other sins. Now yield all parts of your body only to what is good, so that you may become holy. ²⁰ When you were slaves of sin, you felt that you were free from right living. ²¹ But what did you get from living in sin? The end of such things was death. You are ashamed of them now. ²² But since you have been set free from sin and have become slaves of God, see what you get in return! You are made holy, and in the end you get everlasting life. ²³ Sin pays death as its wages, but God gives us the free gift of everlasting life if we take Jesus Christ as our Lord.

7 Brethren, I speak to you who know the law. You know that the law has a hold on a person as long as he lives. ² For example, a married woman is bound by law to her husband as long as he lives. But if her husband dies she is free from the law about her husband. ³ If she lives with another man while her husband lives, she will be called a bad woman. But if her husband dies she is free from that law. Then if she marries another man, she is not a bad woman. ⁴ In the same way, when the body of Christ died, you too died; you died to the law of Moses. Now you belong to another. You belong to Him who has been raised from the dead.

Now we can bear fruit for God. [5] While we were living for our flesh the law made our evil passions even worse. [6] But now we are freed from the law. We died to that sin which once had us in its power. We no longer serve under the old written law. Now we live this new life under God's Spirit.

[7] Can we say then that the law is sin? Certainly not! But the law reveals our sins to us. If it had not been for the law I should not have known what sin is. If the law had not said "You shall not covet," I would not have known what it is to covet. [8] But when the command not to covet came, I realized how much I was sinning. I knew that I was coveting in all kinds of ways. When there is no law against a sin, the sense of sin lies dead. [9] When I was a child I was alive, for I did not know the law. But when the commands came, sin came to life in me and I died. [10] The very commands that promised life proved to be death to me, because I broke them. [11] Sin found its chance in the commands. It deceived me and killed me. [12] But the law itself is holy, and the commands are holy and just and good.

[13] Did that good law then bring death to me? Certainly not. It was not the law, it was the sin that worked death in me, by making me break that good law. This is how sin was shown to be sin. The commands only revealed how terrible sin is. [14] The law belongs to the spirit—we know that. But I am made of flesh and am sold as a slave to sin. [15] I cannot understand my own actions. I do not do what I want to do, but I do the very things I hate. [16] But if I do what I do not want to do, I agree that the law is right. [17] It is no longer I that do evil, but sin living in me. [18] I know that nothing good lives in my flesh. I intend to do what is right, but I do not do it. [19] I do not do the good I want to do, but I do the evil that I do not want to do. [20] If I do what I do not want to do, it is not I that do it, but sin living in me.

[21] I find it to be a law of my nature that when I want to do

right, evil is still with me. [22] For I delight in the law of God down in my soul. [23] But I see in my body another law at war with the law of my mind. That law of my body makes me a prisoner to sin which is in my body. [25a] The best I can do by myself is to serve the law of God with my mind, but the law of sin with my flesh. [24] Unhappy man that I am, who will set me free from this death-bound body? [25b] Thanks be to God Who sent Jesus Christ our Lord. He has set me free.

8   There is now no sentence of death for those who are in Christ Jesus. [2] The Spirit has its own law, and this law gives me life in Christ Jesus. It sets me free from sin and death. [3] What the law of Moses could not do because our flesh was too weak, God has done. He sent His Son in flesh like our sinning flesh. Christ died as a sin-offering for us. In this way God passed a death sentence upon sin in the flesh. [4] Now we are able to live as the just law requires if we obey the Spirit and do not obey the call of the flesh.

[5] Those who live for the Spirit keep their minds on the things of the Spirit. Those who live for the flesh keep their minds on the things of the flesh. [6] To keep the mind on the flesh means death. But to keep the mind on the Spirit means life and peace. [7] The mind that is set on the flesh is the enemy of God. It does not and cannot obey the law of God. [8] Those who live for the flesh cannot please God.

[9] But you do not live for the flesh. You live for the Spirit, if the Spirit of God really lives in you. Any man who does not have the Spirit of Christ does not belong to Christ. [10] If Christ lives in you, your bodies are dead because of sin, but your spirits are alive and you love what is right. [11] The Spirit of God who raised Jesus from the dead lives in you. And God is going to put life into your bodies just as He raised Christ Jesus from the dead. It is His Spirit which lives in you which will be your life.

[12] So then, brothers, we do not owe a duty to the flesh. We are not to obey the call of the flesh. [13] If you live for the flesh

you will die. But if you are led by the Spirit, and put to death the deeds of the body, you will live. [14] For all those who are led by God's Spirit are God's sons. [15] You did not receive the spirit of a slave, to make you fear. But you have received the spirit of a Son of God. That is why we cry, "Father, dear Father." [16] The Spirit of God is bearing witness with our spirits that we are children of God. [17] If we are God's children we are also to be God's heirs. We are fellow-heirs with Christ. If we share His sufferings, we shall also share His glory. [18] I do not consider the sufferings of this present time worth comparing to the glory that is going to be revealed to us.

[19] Even the created world is waiting with eager desire for the sons of God to appear. [20] Every created thing has been put under the power of death and decay. Nothing wants to die or decay, but God has willed it so. Yet He gave us hope [21] that the created world itself will be set free from decay and death. Then everything in the world will obtain the glorious liberty of the children of God. [22] We know that the whole created world has been groaning in the pains of childbirth until now. [23a] Not only the world around us, but we ourselves have been groaning within. We are waiting for God to deliver our bodies from the power of death. We are waiting for Him to adopt us as His sons. [24] This is the hope that saves us. If it had already happened we would not need to hope for it. Who hopes for a thing after he has it? [25] But if we still hope for what we do not yet see, we must be patient while we wait for it.

[23b] The Holy Spirit is a glorious first fruit of what God plans to give us. [26] The Holy Spirit helps us, because we are weak. We do not know how we ought to pray. But the Holy Spirit Himself keeps praying for us with sighs too deep for words. [27] God Who can see into men's hearts, knows what the Spirit desires. And the Spirit keeps praying for God's people in the way God wishes. [28] We know that God works with those who love Him to bring good out of everything.

Those who love Him have been called according to His purpose. [29] He knew them before they were born and He had chosen them to become like His son. Jesus was the first born and those whom God has chosen are His brothers. [30] Those whom God chose He called. He cleared all charges against those whom He called. He gave His own glory to those whose charges He cleared.

[31] What then can we say if this is true? God is for us, so who can be against us? [32] God did not spare His own Son, but gave Him up for us all. And God will gladly give us all things along with Christ. [33] Who then shall bring any charges against those whom God has chosen? It was God Who cleared their charges, so who dares to condemn them? [34] Christ Jesus died; He was raised from the dead; He is at the right hand of God. And it is He who pleads for us. [35] Who shall separate us from the love of Christ? Shall trouble or pain or ill treatment or hunger or need of clothes or danger or death? [36] As it is written:

> "For Thy sake we face death the whole day;
> we are regarded as sheep to be killed."

[37] Yet in all these things that happen we shall have victory and more than victory by the help of Him Who loved us. [38] I am sure that nothing shall be able to separate us from Christ, in life or in death. Neither angels nor even the princes of the dark spirit world can separate us from Christ. Nothing now and nothing that shall ever come, can separate us. [39] No power, no height, no depth, nor anything God has created will be able to separate us from His love which He gave us in Christ Jesus our Lord.

9 [1-3] I have great sorrow and pain in my heart all the time about my own brothers of the Jewish race who refused Christ. I would be willing to be under a curse and to be cut off from Christ for their sakes. This is the truth. Christ and my conscience and the Holy Spirit bear me witness that I am not lying. [4] They are Israelites: they have a right to the glory of sons. They were bound by an agreement with God. The Law of Moses was given to them. They have the worship and the promises. [5] The early

fathers were theirs. Christ in His flesh was of their race. May God Who is over all be blessed for ever! Amen!

⁶ I do not mean to say that God's word failed. It did not fail among the Jews whom He had chosen. God did not choose all the children of Jacob as His true "Israel." ⁷ᵃ God did not choose all who descended from Abraham as the true "children of Abraham." Abraham had children whom God did not choose. ⁹ When Abraham was an old man, God promised him another son. God said:

> "In about a year from now I will come back to you, and then your wife Sarah will have a son."

⁷ᵇ God kept that promise and Sarah gave birth to Isaac. Then God told Abraham:

> "The children of Isaac, not your other children, shall be My chosen people."

⁸ This means that nobody can claim to be a child of God just because his parents were children of God. It means that each of us must put his faith in God's promises.

¹⁰ And we cannot put our faith in our own good works, but only in God's mercy. What God said to Isaac proves this. Isaac's wife Rebecca had two babies in her body at the same time, both of them sons of Isaac. ¹² God said to Isaac:

> "The older son Esau shall serve the younger son Jacob."

¹³ And God's word says:

> "I chose Jacob, but I did not choose Esau."

¹¹ Those boys were not yet born, so they had never done anything either good or bad. This proves that God does not choose men because of their good works. God selects and calls them to suit His own deep secret purposes.

¹⁴ Now what shall we say? That God is not just? No, we cannot say that. ¹⁵ For He said to Moses, "I will have mercy on

those on whom I wish to show mercy. I will pity those whom I wish to pity." [16] So it depends upon God's mercy. It does not depend upon what a man wants or what he does. [17] The Holy Writings prove this, where God said to Pharaoh: "I have raised you up for a purpose. I am using you to show My power. Through you, My name shall be made known in all the world." [18] So we see that God has mercy on anybody when He wishes. And He makes a man's heart hard if He wishes it to be so.

[19] You may say to me: "Why then does God still find fault? For who can oppose His will?" [20] But, man, are you wise enough to answer back to God? If a man makes a pot, will the pot say, "Why have you made me like this?" [21] Doesn't a man have a right to make what he pleases out of clay? He can make of the same lump of clay one vessel for beauty and another vessel for some low use. [22] Are we not like clay in God's hands? We can only guess why He made us as we are. It may be that God desires to show His power. Who knows? It may be that He wants to show His anger at sin. It may be that He made some vessels intending to destroy them. Who knows? Perhaps He is only being patient with those vessels a little longer. [23] It may be that He wishes to show the wealth of His glory to the vessels which He made for mercy, and which He intended for His glory. [24] Nobody knows God's secret purposes. But we do know that we are among those vessels which He called for mercy. He called some of us from among the Jews and some of us from among the Gentiles. [25] Indeed He says in Hosea:

> "Those who were not My people
> I will call 'My People,'
> and I will love her
> whom I did not love before."

[26] God says to the Gentiles:

> "You are not My people,"

29

But in the very same place He says about the Gentiles:

> "They shall be called
> 'sons of the living God.' "

27 But concerning Israel this is what Isaiah cried:

> "The number of the sons of Israel is like the
> sands of the sea.
> Yet only a small part of them will be saved.
> 28 With speed and power the Lord will carry out
> His sentence upon the earth."

29 Isaiah says that some of Israel will be saved:

> "If the Lord of hosts had not left us some children,
> we would all have been destroyed like Sodom
> and Gomorrah."

30 This then we can say: Although the Gentiles did not try to be just under the law, nevertheless many of them have been counted just, because of their faith. 31 But Israel tried to be just by obeying the law and did not succeed. 32 Why did the Jews not succeed? Because they did not try to be just through faith, but through obeying the law of Moses. They stumbled over that stone of which God speaks 33 in His Word:

> "Look, I am laying in Zion a stone that will make
> men trip.
> It is a rock that will make them fall.
> But the man who believes in Him shall not be
> put to shame."

10 Brothers, my heart desires that all the Jews should be saved, and I keep praying to God for them. 2 I will say this in their defense: They are eager for God, but they do not understand His ways. 3 They do not know the true way to become right with God. They do not depend upon God's mercy but try

to prove that they have kept the law. [5] They depend upon Moses who said:

"A man shall live if he does what the law commands."

[4] But Christ has put an end to the old law. Now every one who has faith in Christ shall be counted just in the sight of God. [6] Now you are right with God. Christ is in your very heart. You need not ask yourself:

"Who will go up to heaven and bring Christ down?"

[7] And you need not ask:

"Who will go and bring Christ up from the dead?"

[8] For see what it says:

"The Word is near you.
It is in your mouth and in your heart."

This "Word" is the faith which we are preaching. [9] If you confess with your mouth that Jesus is Lord, and believe in your heart that God raised Him from the dead, you shall be saved. [10] In his heart a man believes, and then he is counted just. And with his mouth a man confesses and is saved. [11] The Holy Writings say:

"No one who believes in Him shall ever be put
to shame."

[12] The Lord treats the Jew and the Gentile just alike. The same Lord is Lord of them all. He pours out His riches upon all who call upon Him for help. [13] So it is written,

"Every one who calls upon the name of the Lord
will be saved."

[14] But how can they call upon Him if they do not believe in Him? And how can they believe in Him if they have not heard

about Him? And how can they hear about Him if nobody tells them? [15] And how can anybody tell them if he is not sent? This is why it is written:

> "How beautiful are the feet of those who bring good
> news."

[17] Faith comes only when people have heard. And they hear only when somebody preaches about Christ.

[18] But I ask you: Did they not have a chance to hear men preach? Certainly they did. One of the Psalms says of those who preached:

> "Their voice has gone out into all the earth,
> and their words to the furthest parts of this world."

[16] But not all the people were willing to listen to the Good News. Isaiah says,

> "Lord, who has heard and believed what we told
> them?"

[19] So we ask: Why did not Israel believe? Did they not understand? The answer is: They refused to understand.

So God went to the Gentiles. Moses tells us that God did this to make Israel jealous:

> "I will make you jealous," God says, "of people
> who are not a nation.
> I will make you angry when I call a nation you
> look down upon."

[20] Isaiah dares to say for God:

> "I have been found by men who did not seek for
> me.
> I have shown myself to those who did not ask
> for me."

²¹ But of Israel, Isaiah says,

> "All day long I held out my hand to a contrary
> people who refused to obey."

11 Again I ask this question: Has God cast off His people? No, not at all. I myself am a son of Israel, a child of Abraham. I am a member of the tribe of Benjamin. ² God has not cast off those whom He has always known and chosen. Have you read in the Holy Writings what Elijah said to God against Israel?

> ³ "Lord, they have killed Your prophets.
> They have destroyed Your altars.
> I alone am left, and they seek my life."

⁴ But Elijah was mistaken. There were many others whom God had chosen. Here is what God replied:

> "I have kept for myself seven thousand men who
> have not bowed the knee to Baal."

⁵ And again at the present time there are many in Israel whom God chose in His loving kindness. ⁶ But it was only through His loving kindness that He chose them. They did not earn His choice by their good works. If they had earned it, we could not call it God's "free gift."

⁷ This then is what I have explained. Many sons of Israel failed to obtain what they were seeking. Only those whom God chose obtained it. The rest were made hard and could not understand. ⁸ It was written of them:

> God gave them a dull spirit like one asleep.
> He gave them eyes that could not see,
> and ears that could not hear
> down to this very day.

⁹ And David said:

> "Let their holy feast become a net and a trap;
> let it be a hole into which they will fall and
> be punished;

33

¹⁰ let their eyes become so poor that they can-
not see;
let their backs be bent for ever."

¹¹ That makes us ask: Does this mean they have fallen and
been ruined for ever? No, it does not mean that. It means that
through Israel's sin, the Gentiles have been saved. This will make
Israel jealous, so that Israel will want to be saved too. ¹² Think
of that! Israel's sin made the whole world rich. Their failing to
accept God's gift made the Gentiles rich. Just think how much
more it will mean when they all come in too!

¹³ Now I shall speak to you Gentiles. As an apostle to you
Gentiles, I am trying to bring as many of you to Christ as
possible. ¹⁴ I hope this will make my fellow Jews jealous, and
thus save some of them. ¹⁵ Their being shut out has meant that
many others in the world are being made right with God. See
what it will mean when they also are accepted! It will be like
life coming from the dead!

¹⁶ In the temple the priest offers a handful of dough to God,
and that makes all the dough holy. If the root of the tree is holy
its branches are holy. Israel still has a holy root.

¹⁷ But some of Israel's branches were cut off. You Gentiles
were grafted in their place like a wild olive shoot. You are sharing the rich growth of the olive tree. ¹⁸ But don't boast that you
are better than the cut-off branches. If you feel proud, remember that you do not support the root. It is the root that supports
you. ¹⁹ You may say, "Those branches have been cut off so that
I might be grafted in." ²⁰ That is true: they were cut off because
they did not have faith. And you stay fast to the branch only
because you have faith. So do not become proud. Rather, be
afraid of falling away. ²¹ For God did not spare the natural
branches, so neither will He spare you. ²² You must realize that
God is kind but He is also severe. He is severe toward those
who fall away. But to you He is kind if you continue to trust
His kindness. If you do not, you will be cut off also.

²³ The Jews will also be grafted in once more if they stop refusing to believe. God has the power to graft them in again. ²⁴ You Gentiles were cut from an olive tree that is by nature wild. You were grafted onto a garden tree, although this is against nature. How easily then will the Jews, who are the natural branches, be grafted back into their own olive tree!

²⁵ My brothers, I was afraid you might become wise in your own eyes. So I wanted you to understand this mystery: a part of Israel has become hard, until the full number of the Gentiles come in. ²⁶ Then all of Israel too will be saved. For it is written,

> "From Zion will come the man to save her.
> He will put an end to Jacob's sinning against
> God."

God says,

> ²⁷ "This will be my binding promise to them
> when I take away their sins."

²⁸ So then those Jews who refuse to believe the Good News still remain God's enemies, while you Gentiles are becoming God's friends. Yet God still loves the Jews for the sake of their fathers and He has chosen them too. They are still His chosen people. ²⁹ When God calls men and offers them His gifts, He never changes His mind.

³⁰ In the past you did not obey God. But now you have received God's mercy, while those others whom He chose still refuse to obey Him. ³¹ The Jews refuse to obey, but God's mercy to you will some day make them turn to Him. Then the Jews too will receive His mercy. ³² God has condemned all men alike, Jews and Gentiles, for breaking His law; but He will have mercy upon them all alike.

³³ Oh, how deep is the mind of God! Oh, how rich are His wisdom and knowledge! How impossible it is to read His thoughts! How impossible it is to understand His ways!

³⁴ "Who has known the mind of the Lord?
Whom has He asked for advice?
³⁵ Who has given Him a gift,
that God could pay back?"

³⁶ From Him come all things. Through His power all things continue. For Him all things were made. To Him be the glory for ever. Amen.

12 I appeal to you, brothers, since God has shown such mercies to you, offer up your bodies as a living sacrifice. Keep your bodies holy so that God can accept them. This is the way to worship in the Spirit. ² Do not be like the world, but let Christ change your life and give you a new mind. Then you will be able to know what is the will of God, what is good, what God accepts, and what is perfect.

³ I am writing to you by the grace God gave me. And I bid every one of you not to think better of himself than he ought to think. Think with sound judgment. Let each man's work measure up to the faith which God has given him. ⁴ In our bodies there are many members and not all the members have the same work to do. ⁵ So we who are in Christ are many members. Yet we are all the same body. Each one of us really belongs to all the rest of us. ⁶ We have different kinds of gifts which God in His grace gave us. Let us use them. If we have a gift for telling God's will, let us use it as far as our faith carries us. ⁷ If our gift is service, let us serve. If we have a gift of teaching, let us teach. ⁸ If our gift is speaking, let us use it for Christ. He who gives, let him give with a big heart. He who helps others, let him do it with all his might. He who does acts of mercy, let him do them with joy.

⁹ Let your love be real. Hate all evil. Hold fast to all that is good. ¹⁰ Love one another as brothers ought to love. Do your best to show honor to one another. ¹¹ And do not let your love for Christ's work grow cold. Be on fire with the Spirit, as you

serve the Lord. ¹²Let your hope fill you with joy. Be patient when troubles come. Be praying constantly. ¹³Give to the saints who need help. Welcome strangers into your homes.

¹⁴Bless those who ill treat you. Bless them and do not curse them. ¹⁵Be glad with those who are glad. Weep with those who weep. ¹⁶Live in peace and good will toward one another. Do not be proud. Associate with humble people. Never be vain. ¹⁷Never pay back evil for evil. Always remember to do what is noble in the sight of all men. ¹⁸If possible, as far as it depends on you, live at peace with all men. ¹⁹My dear friends, never strike back at one who harms you. Leave that to the anger of God. For it is written,

> Punishment is for me to give.
> I will pay back, says the Lord.

²⁰No, if your enemy is hungry, feed him. If he needs water, give him drink. When you do that, you will heap burning coals upon his head. ²¹Do not be defeated by evil, but defeat evil with good.

13 Let every person obey the government authorities. For there is no authority except from God. Those in authority have been appointed by God. ²So if anybody opposes the authorities, he opposes what God has appointed. If he opposes them, he will bring judgment on himself. ³Those who rule are not a terror to good men but to bad. If you do not wish to be afraid of a man in authority, do right, and he will approve of you. ⁴He is God's servant to do you good. But if you do wrong, be afraid of him. For he does not carry his sword for nothing. He is the servant of God to punish the man who does wrong. ⁵You must obey the authorities, not only to escape punishment, but also for the sake of your conscience. ⁶This is why you ought also to pay your taxes. The authorities are the officers of God to take care of these things. ⁷Pay them whatever is due them. Pay taxes to whom taxes are due. Show respect to those to whom respect is due. Honor those to whom honor is due. [8] Owe no one anything, except to love one another. For he who loves his neighbor has carried out the law. [9] The commands of God say:

> "You must not take another man's wife. You must not kill. You must not steal. You must not covet what belongs to another."

These and the other commands are all summed up in this one sentence:

> "You must love your neighbor as you love yourself."

[10] Love never wrongs a neighbor, and so love carries out the law.

[11] You know what time it is. It is time for you to wake up. The time when we all shall be saved is much nearer than it was when we first accepted Christ. [12] The night is gone; the day is here. So let us stop doing what we did in the darkness. Let us clothe ourselves for the light of the new day. [13] Let our conduct be fitting for this new day. Keep away from drinking parties with loud talk and disgusting actions and loose sex morals. Never quarrel. Never be jealous. Be clothed with the Lord Jesus Christ. Make no plans to satisfy the desires of the flesh.

14 If a man is weak in faith, welcome him. Do not have any arguments with him over his beliefs. [2] One man believes he may eat everything. But another man with weak faith eats only vegetables. [3] Let him who eats meat not look down upon him who does not eat meat. Let him who eats no meat not pass judgment on him who does eat meat. God has accepted him and he is God's servant. [4] Who are you to pass judgment on the servant of another? It is before his own Master God that he must stand or fall. And I am sure a man is going to stand whether he eats meat or not, for the Master is able to help him stand.

[5] One man regards one day as better than other days. Another man regards all days alike. That is all right, providing

each man is quite sure in his own mind. ⁶ The man who observes special days, does so to honor the Lord. He who eats meat, does it to honor the Lord, for he gives thanks to God. The other does not eat meat, so that he may honor the Lord, and he also gives thanks to God.

⁷ None of us lives for himself alone and none of us dies alone. ⁸ If we live we live for the Lord. And if we die we die for the Lord. So whether we live or die, we belong to the Lord. ⁹ Christ died and came to life again. By doing that he became Lord and judge of both the dead and the living.

¹⁰ Why, then, do you try to be judge of your brother? Why do you look down on your brother? We all shall have to stand before the judgment seat of God. ¹¹ For it is written:

"As I live, says the Lord, every knee shall bow to Me
and every tongue shall give praise to God."

¹² Each of us therefore will have to answer for himself to God.

¹³So let us not pass judgment on one another any more. Let us never put a block in the path of a brother to trip him up. ¹⁴ I myself am sure that for those who are in the Lord Jesus, nothing is wrong to eat. I am sure of that. And yet it is wrong for a man to eat a thing if he thinks it is wrong. ¹⁵ If your brother is being hurt by what you eat, then you are no longer walking in love. Do not allow what you eat to ruin one for whom Christ died. ¹⁶ Do not let what is good for you get a bad name. ¹⁷ The kingdom of God does not mean food and drink. It means right living and peace and joy in the Holy Spirit. ¹⁸ He who serves Christ in that good spirit is accepted by God and he is approved by man. ¹⁹ Let us then aim at peace and try to build up one another. ²⁰ Let us not for the sake of eating food destroy the work of God. Even though all kinds of food are right for you to eat, yet it is wrong for you to make another man fall by what you eat. ²¹ It is not right for you to eat meat or drink wine or do anything that makes your brother fall. ²² Keep your own faith about eating foods, but keep it between yourself and God. Happy is a

man if he has no doubts about what is right for him to do.
²³ But he who has doubts about eating meat is condemned if he
eats it, because he does not believe that what he is doing is right.
When you do what you do not believe to be right, you sin.

15 We who have strong faith ought to bear with the failings of
those who have weak faith. We should not just please ourselves.
² Let each of us try to please his neighbor. Let us do him good
by building up his faith. ³ Christ did not please Himself. It is
written,

> "The cruel words of those who spoke evil against
>   you fell on Me."

⁴ What was written in the old days was meant to teach us
today. God through His Holy Writings encourages us to be
patient and to keep hoping. ⁵ God will help you stand firm and
will encourage you. May He also help you to live in harmony
with one another, as Jesus Christ desires you to live. ⁶ May you
all together sing to the glory of God the Father of our Lord
Jesus Christ. ⁷ And for the glory of God welcome every brother
in Christ, whether Jew or Gentile, for Christ has welcomed you
all. ⁸ As I told you, Christ first came to the circumcised Jews.
This showed that God had told the truth. For God had promised
our Jewish fathers that Christ should come to them. ⁹ But Christ
has also come to the Gentiles. For this reason the Gentiles are
praising God for His mercy. It is written:

> "This is why I will praise Thee among the Gentiles
>   and sing to Thy name."

¹⁰ and again it is written:

> "Be glad, O Gentiles, along with the people of God."

¹¹ and again:

> "Praise the Lord, all Gentiles.
>   Let all the peoples praise Him."

¹² And again Isaiah says:

> "From the family tree of Jesse shall grow up a root.
> He will rise to rule the Gentiles,
> in Him will the Gentiles put their hope."

¹³ You Gentiles have believed God. He has given you this hope. May He fill you with joy and peace. And may your hope overflow by the power of the Holy Spirit.

¹⁴ I am sure, my brothers, that you are living good lives. I am sure you have learned what you need to know about Christ, and are able to teach one another. ¹⁵ But I have dared to write to you and remind you about some points. ¹⁶ I dared to write because God in His grace made me a minister to the Gentiles. I am His priest in the service of God's good news. As His priest I am offering the Gentiles to God. The Holy Spirit will make them holy so that God can accept them. ¹⁷ I am proud of my work for God under Christ Jesus. ¹⁸ I am most proud of what Christ has done through me to win the Gentiles to obey Him. He has worked through me by word and deed. ¹⁹ He did this by the power of signs and wonders, and by the power of the Holy Spirit. From Jerusalem all the way around to Illyricum I have preached the good news of Christ. ²⁰ I try always to go and preach the good news where Christ has not yet been named. I do not wish to build on another man's foundation. ²¹ In this I am following what Isaiah has written:

> They, who were not told, shall now see!
> They, who have not heard, shall understand!

²² My work up to now has prevented me from coming to you. ²³But now there are no longer fresh fields for me to enter in this part of the world. For many years I have longed to visit you. ²⁴ So I hope to see you at last as I pass through Rome on the way to Spain. And I hope you will see me off on my journey after I have enjoyed being with you for a while.

[25] At present, however, I am going to Jerusalem with aid for God's people there. [26] I am going because the churches in Macedonia and Greece have decided to send a gift for the poor Christians in Jerusalem. [27] They were glad to do it. Indeed they are in debt to them. They and all the Gentiles are sharing the blessings of the Spirit which came to them through the Jews. So they feel it is their duty to give material help. [28] I am going to make this trip to Jerusalem and deliver to them what has been collected. After that I shall go to Spain by way of Rome. [29] I know that when I come to you I shall come with the full blessing of Christ.

[30] Brothers, I beg you to pray hard for me as I go to Jerusalem. I appeal to you in the name of our Lord Jesus Christ. [31] Pray that I may not be harmed in Judea by those men who deny our Good News. Pray that God's people in Jerusalem may accept my services. [32] Then, God willing, I shall be happy to come and rest in your company. [33] Now may the God of peace be with you all. Amen.

16 Let me introduce sister Phoebe to you. She is serving in the church at Cenchreae. [2] Welcome her in the way followers of the Lord should welcome one another. Give her whatever help she may need. She has helped me and many other people.

[3] I send my greetings to Prisca and Aquila, my fellow workers for Christ Jesus. [4] They risked their lives to save my life. I thank them and so do all the Gentile churches. [5] My greetings also to the church which meets in their house. My greetings to my dear friend, Epaenetus, who was the first man in Asia to turn to Christ. [6] My greetings to Mary, who has worked hard for you. [7] Greetings to Andronicus and Junias, who belong to my own country and who once went to prison with me. They are well known among the apostles, and they began to follow Christ before I did. [8] I also send greetings to Ampliatus, my dear friend in the Lord. [9] My greetings to Urbanus, our fellow worker in Christ, and to my friend Stachys. [10] I greet Apelles, who is

approved by Christ. And I greet all who belong to the family of Aristobulus. [11] I greet Herodion, who is also from my country. I send my greetings to those in the family of Narcissus who are in the Lord. [12] I greet Tryphaena and Tryphosa who work hard for the Lord. And I greet my dear sister Persis. She has been a hard worker in the Lord's service. [13] I greet Rufus, one of God's chosen ones, and his mother, who has been a mother to me. [14] I send greetings to Asyncritus, Phelgon, Hermes, Patrobas, Hermas and the brothers who meet with them. [15] My greetings to Philologus, Julia, Nereus and his sister, and also to Olympas and all God's people who meet with them. [16] Greet one another for me with a holy kiss. All the churches of Christ send greetings.

[17] Brothers, I urge you to watch out for those who cause quarrels and difficulties, and who oppose what you have been taught. Avoid those men. [18] Such persons are not serving our Lord Christ. They are serving their own stomachs. By their smooth words of praise, they deceive simple-minded people.

[19] Every one reports how you have obeyed the commands of Christ. I am greatly pleased about this. I hope you will always remain wise about good but innocent about evil. [20] The God of peace will soon crush Satan under your feet. May the grace of our Lord Jesus be with you.

[21] Timothy, my fellow worker sends greetings to you and so do Lucius and Jason and Sosipater, who came from my country.

[22] I, Tertius, have written this letter for Paul as he told me what to write. I send my greetings in the Lord. [23] I am the guest of Gaius, and the church meets in his home. Gaius wishes to be remembered to you. Erastus the city treasurer sends his greetings, and so does brother Quartus.

[25] And now, I, Paul, am closing this letter. Through the Good News about Jesus Christ, God is able to make you strong Christians. In this letter I have explained to you the great mystery about Jesus Christ. The ever-living God has kept it secret through the ages. [26] But he has now revealed it through His prophets. Now He has commanded us to let all the nations know the

secret. He desires every nation to have faith in Christ and to obey Him. ²⁷ To the only wise God be glory for ever through Jesus Christ. Amen.

Paul

PAUL'S FIRST LETTER
TO THE CHRISTIANS IN CORINTH

From: *Paul, whom God appointed as an apostle of Jesus Christ and our brother Sosthenes*

To: *The Church of God in Corinth:*

1 I write to you who have been made holy by Christ Jesus. You have been called to be God's people. ² I also write this letter for all those who in any place pray in the name of the Lord Jesus Christ. He is their Lord and ours. ³ I wish you grace and peace from God our Father and the Lord Jesus Christ.

⁴ God has wonderful loving kindness. That is why He gave you Jesus Christ. For this I always keep thanking Him. ⁵ He has made your lives rich in every way. He has given you complete understanding of our faith, and the gift of explaining it to others. ⁶ All that I promised Christ would do for you has come true!

⁷ You do not lack any gift that the Spirit can give you. Now you are waiting for the day when the Lord Jesus Christ will appear. ⁸ He will keep you strong while you wait. On the day when our Lord Jesus Christ comes you will be cleared of every sin. ⁹ God has called you into the family circle of His Son Jesus Christ our Lord and He is faithful.

¹⁰ But brothers, I beg you in the name of the Lord Jesus Christ to agree among yourselves. There must be no divisions among you. You must be united. You must all have the same

mind and the same purpose. [11] I say this, brothers, because Chloe's people have reported to me that there is quarreling among you. [12] I mean this: One of you says: "I belong to Paul." Another says: "I belong to Apollos." Another says: "I belong to Peter." Another says: "I belong to Christ." [13] Is Christ divided? Did Paul die on the cross for you? Was it in Paul's name that you were baptized? [14] I am glad now that I baptized none of you excepting Crispus and Gaius. [15] Then no one can say that you were baptized in my name. [16] Yes, I now remember that I did baptize Stephanas' family. But I do not remember anybody else whom I baptized. [17] Christ did not send me to baptize. He sent me to you to preach the Good News. I did not use fine language when I was with you. I did not want the cross of Christ to lose its power in wise sounding words. [18] The story of the cross sounds foolish to people who are on the way to destruction. But to us who are being saved, the cross is the power of God.

[19] It is written:

> "I will destroy the wisdom of the wise.
> And I will show how false are the bright ideas of
>   the wise men."

[20] I ask you: Where are those wise men now? Where are those writers? Where are the men who love to defend the "wisdom" of this age? God has shown that all the world's wisdom is foolish. [21] God did not allow the world with its supposed wisdom to understand His true wisdom. But God in His wisdom is pleased to save every one of us who believes the Good News. This Good News which we preach about Christ is so simple that wise men of this world call it foolish. [22] The Jews want to see signs, and the Greeks seek "wisdom." [23] But we preach only that Christ died on the cross for us. That message is shocking to the Jews and it seems very foolish to the Gentiles. [24] But every one whom God calls, whether Jew or Greek, knows that Christ is the power and the wisdom of God. [25] So God's plan, which many

call "foolish," is wiser than the wisest plans of men. And God's method, which many call "weak," is stronger than the strongest methods of men.

²⁶ Brothers, think who you were when God called you. Not many of you were what men considered wise. Not many of you had positions of power. Not many of you were of noble birth.

²⁷ God chose the common people of the world to shame the wise. He chose the weak to shame the strong. ²⁸ He chose the low people whom others looked down upon. He chose those whom proud people thought were nobody. He did this to show those who thought they were important that they were nothing. ²⁹ He did this so that no human being might boast in God's presence. ³⁰ It was God who gave us the new life we have in Christ Jesus. God gave us Christ to be our wisdom. It was Christ who made us right with God. It was Christ who made us holy. It was Christ who saved us from our sins. ³¹ Therefore, as it is written:

"Let him who boasts, boast about the Lord."

2   When I first came to you, brothers, I explained to you God's secret purpose. But I tried not to tell it in words difficult to understand. ² I decided that while I was with you I would forget everything but Christ Jesus and His death on the cross for us. ³ In truth I was weak and trembling and afraid when I visited you. ⁴ When I talked I did not depend upon words of wisdom to persuade you. The proof of what I said was God's spirit and power. ⁵ I spoke this way so that your faith would not rest on the wisdom of men, but on the power of God.

⁶ There is a kind of wisdom which we explain to those who are full-grown in faith. But it is not what this world calls wisdom. It is not what the rulers of today call wisdom. Those rulers will soon be gone. ⁷ But the wisdom that we speak of is from God. It is wisdom about the hidden secret plan which God formed for our glory before the ages began. ⁸ The rulers of this world have never understood this plan. If they had understood it they

would not have nailed the Lord of glory to the cross. ⁹ But as
it is written, there are things

"Which no eye ever saw, and no ear ever heard.
There are things which never entered the mind of man.
These things God prepared for those who love Him."

¹⁰ God has revealed these things to us through His Spirit. Nothing is hidden from the Spirit, not even the deep wisdom of God.
¹¹ Nobody really knows a man's thoughts except that man's own
spirit. It is far more certain that nobody can really know the
thoughts of God except God's own Spirit. ¹² God's own Spirit
is what we have received, not the spirit of the world. That is why
we can understand God's gifts to us. ¹³ We teach this to others,
not in words of human wisdom, but in words taught us by the
Spirit. We explain the Spirit's truths in the Spirit's language.

¹⁴ A man without God's Spirit does not accept these gifts
which come from the Spirit of God. To him they are foolish gifts,
for he is not able to understand them. The reason is that they
must be seen with the eyes of the Spirit. ¹⁵ The man who has the
Spirit can see the meaning of it all. But no one who does not
have God's Spirit is able to judge us who have God's Spirit. ¹⁶ As
God's Word says,

"Who has known the mind of the Lord?
Who can teach Him?"

But we have shared the very thoughts of Christ!

3 When I came to Corinth, brothers, I could not talk to you
as men full-grown in the Spirit. I had to treat you as men of
the world who were still only babies in the knowledge of Christ.
² I had to feed you with milk. You were not ready for solid
food.

And even yet you cannot take solid food. ³ You are still men
of the world. So long as you are jealous of one another and
quarrel with one another, you are led by the flesh the same as
ordinary men. ⁴ For when one says, "I belong to Paul," and

another says, "I belong to Apollos," you are exactly like men of the world.

⁵ Who is Apollos? Who is Paul? He and I are only servants used by God to help you believe in Christ. Each of us is doing what the Lord gave us to do. ⁶ I planted and Apollos watered, but God made you grow. ⁷ He then who plants and he who waters count for nothing, but only God counts who is making you grow. ⁸ The man who plants and the man who waters are equals. Each of us will be paid for his own work. ⁹ We both work together for God. You are God's field.

Or, to say it another way, you are God's house which we are building. ¹⁰ By the grace of God I was able to lay the foundation like an expert worker. Another man is building the house on that foundation. But every man must take care how he builds upon it. ¹¹ Christ Jesus himself is the foundation. No one can lay any other foundation. ¹² One man may build on the foundation with gold or silver or precious stones. Another may build with wood or hay or straw. ¹³ The day of judgment will show what materials each man used. When that day comes, a fire will try each man's building. The fire will prove what kind of work each man did. ¹⁴ If the house which he built on the foundation remains standing, he shall receive his pay. ¹⁵ But if the man's work is burned up he will lose everything. Although he will be saved, it will be through fire.

¹⁶ Do you know that you are God's temple? Do you realize that God's Spirit makes His home in you? ¹⁷ If any one destroys God's temple, God will destroy him. God's temple is holy and you are that holy temple. ¹⁸ Let no one deceive himself about this.

Does any one among you think he is wise with this world's wisdom? He will have to let the world call him a fool before God will call him wise. ¹⁹ For the wisdom of this world is foolish in God's eyes. It is written:

"He catches the wise in their own scheming";

²⁰ and again it is written:

> "The Lord knows that the thinking of the wise will
> end in nothing."

²¹ Never boast that you belong to any man. Everything and everybody belongs to you. ²² Paul and Apollos and Peter belong to you. The whole world, life and death, the present and the future, all belong to you. ²³ And you belong to Christ, and Christ belongs to God.

4 So consider Apollos and me simply as servants of God. God has trusted us to reveal His secret truths to others. ² When God trusts a man to do any work, the man must show God that he is worthy of that trust. ³ It does not matter what you or any human court may think about my work. I dare not even judge myself. ⁴ I do not know of any charge against myself, but that does not clear me. It is the Lord who must judge my work. ⁵ Do not pass any judgment upon my work until the Lord comes. He will bring to light everything that is now hidden in the dark. He will make plain all the purposes in men's hearts. Then God will give every man the praise he deserves.

⁶ I have said these things about Apollos and myself to keep you true to our teaching. I do not want any of you to be vain about belonging to any one of us over against another. ⁷ Who are the men among you who think they are better than the rest of you? What do any of you have that you did not receive? Nothing! You received it all. Why then are you boasting as though it were some virtue of your own, and not a gift?

⁸ Already you say you are so satisfied. You have become so rich! Without any aid you have become like kings! I only wish you really were kings in the Kingdom of God, and that we might share the rule with you!

⁹ For I think that God has made us apostles appear to be below all other people. We apostles are like condemned men who are taken to the arena to die to make sport for others. All the

world of men and angels can watch us being killed. [10] We seem to be fools for Christ, while you boast about being wise. You are strong, but we are weak. You have a good name, but we have shame. [11] At this very moment we are hungry and thirsty. We have poor clothes. We are knocked about. We have no home. [12] We work hard with our own hands. When men curse us, we bless them in return. When they ill-treat us we bear it in silence. [13] When they tell lies against us we try to make peace with them. We are being treated by the world like some dirt and waste to be thrown away.

[14] Now, my dear children, I do not write these things to make you feel ashamed. I write them to help you. [15] Even if you have ten thousand guides in Christ you have only one real father in the faith. I became your father in Christ Jesus when I brought you the Good News of Christ. [16] So follow my example, I urge you.

[17] I have sent Timothy to tell you all these things. He is my dear faithful child in the Lord. I sent him to help you keep in mind Christ's way of life which I teach the people in all the churches.

[18] I hear that there are some very vain people among you! They act as though they thought I was never coming to Corinth. [19] But I am coming soon if the Lord is willing. Then I will find out about those vain people; I will ask not what they claim to be, but what power they really have. [20] The Kingdom of God is not words; it is power.

[21] So my children, what will you have when I arrive? Shall I come with a stick or with a gentle loving spirit?

5 It is reported that there is one kind of sin going on among you which is not found even among the heathen. They say that a man is actually living with his father's wife! [2] You allow that, and yet you boast! You ought to hang your heads in shame and sorrow. Drive any man who is doing that out from among you.

[3-4] Although I am not with you in body, I am with you in

spirit. And just as though my body were there, in the name of the Lord Jesus I have passed judgment on the man who does such things. You must call a meeting, and I will be there with you in spirit, with all the power of our Lord Jesus. [5] Then you must deliver that man to Satan. Even if his flesh is destroyed, I hope that his spirit may be saved on the day when the Lord Jesus comes.

[6] Certainly you have no reason to boast. Don't you realize that a little yeast will spread through all the dough? [7] Clean out all this old bad yeast. Have only fresh dough with none of the old yeast in it.

Christ, our Passover Lamb, has been sacrificed for us. [8] Let us not keep the feast of the Passover with any of the old yeast of sin and hate. Let us keep the feast by eating the bread without yeast—the bread of a pure and honest life.

[9] I have already written you that you should not associate with men who have bad morals. [10] However, I did not mean heathen whose morals are bad. Of course you cannot refuse to meet people of the world who have bad morals. You cannot stay entirely away from robbers who want to get everything for themselves. You cannot refuse to meet those who worship idols. To do that you would have to leave the world altogether. [11] But I wrote to you not to associate with any one who says he believes in Christ but who has a bad moral life, or who takes everything for himself, or who worships idols, or who gets drunk or curses other people. Do not even eat with such a man.

[12] It is not my business to judge men outside the church. It is those inside the church whom you must judge. [13] God will judge those outside. Drive out that wicked man from among you.

6 If any of you thinks he has been wronged by his neighbor, do you dare go to law before a heathen court? Why don't you go to the people of God? [2] Do you not know that God's people are to be judges of the world? If the world is to be judged by you, are you not fit to try small cases? [3] Don't you know that we are to judge angels as well as the things in this world? ⁴ If, then, you have such ordinary cases to settle, why do you have them tried by men who are not even in the church? ⁵ I ask this to put you to shame. Is it really true that there is not a single wise man among you who could settle differences between one brother and another. ⁶ Is one brother going to law against another brother before a heathen judge? ⁷ To have any cases at all in court against one another is a defeat for you. Why do you not suffer rather than go to court? Why not rather let them rob you?

⁸ I hear that some of you are wronging and even robbing your own brothers in Christ. ⁹ You ought to know that such wicked men shall not have any share in the Kingdom of God. Do not fool yourselves about this.

Those with bad morals, those who worship idols, those who live with other men's wives, men who have sex relations with other men, ¹⁰ those selfish men who get everything for themselves, those who get drunk, those who curse others and those who rob others—none of them shall have a share in God's Kingdom. ¹¹ Some of you were once like that. But you were washed clean. You were made holy. And you became right with God through the Lord Jesus Christ and the Spirit of our God.

¹² Some one may say, "I am free from the old law. Now all things are right for me." Yes, but a great many things are not good for us. It is true that I am no longer a slave to the old law. But now I am not going to become a slave again—a slave to bad habits.

¹³ Some one may say, "Food was made for the stomach and the stomach for food!" That is true. But God will bring to an end both food and the stomach. We do not live to eat.

Our bodies are not meant for sins of sex. Our bodies are meant for the Lord to dwell in. And the Lord wants to dwell in us. ¹⁴ God who raised the Lord to life will also raise us to life by His power. ¹⁵ Do you not know that your bodies are parts of the body of Christ? So would I ever take any part of Christ's body and join it to a loose woman? No, never! [16] Don't you see that he who joins himself to a loose woman becomes one body with her? For it is written: "The two shall become one."

[17] But he who is united to the Lord becomes one with Him in spirit. [18] So keep away from the sins of sex. Every other sin which a man commits is outside his body. But the man with loose morals sins against his own body. [19] Do you not know that your body is a temple for the Holy Spirit who comes from God and dwells within you? You are not your own. [20] You have been bought for a great price. Therefore, let your bodies be an honor to God.

7 Now let me answer the other questions about which you wrote. Yes, it would be a good thing for a man not to get married. [2] Yet moral conditions are very bad today. Every man had better have a wife of his own to avoid being tempted. And every woman had better have a husband of her own. [3] The husband must give his wife what is due her, and the wife must also give her husband what is due him. [4] No wife can do as she pleases with her body; it is for her husband. Also, no husband can do as he pleases with his body; it is for his wife. [5] Do not refuse one another, except perhaps when both agree to stay apart for a time so that you may give yourselves to prayer. Then come together again. This is so that Satan may not tempt you through your want of self-control. [6] In permitting these things I am not saying that I command you to do them. [7] I wish that every one were as I am. But God has made each of us different. He has given some of us one gift and some of us another.

[8] To all who are not married or who are widows I say: It is a good thing for them to remain single as I do. [9] But if they cannot control themselves, they should marry. It is better to marry than to burn with passion.

[10] To the married I give this charge. It is not mine but the Lord's. "A wife should not separate from her husband." [11] But if she does separate herself, she must not marry another man

although she may of course return to her husband. And a husband must not put away his wife.

[12] Concerning married people, I want to say something which the Lord said nothing about. If any brother has a wife who does not believe in Christ, he should not divorce her if she wants to live with him. [13] If a woman has a husband who does not believe in Christ, she should not divorce him, if he wants to live with her. [14] The husband who does not believe is made holy by his Christian wife, and the wife who does not believe is made holy by her Christian husband. If that were not so, your children would not be clean, but as it is they are holy. [15] But if one who does not believe in Christ desires to separate, let him or her do so. In that case the Christian brother (or sister) is not bound. God has called us to live in peace. [16] Wife, how do you know that you may not save your husband? Husband, how do you know that you may not save your wife?

[17] Let every one continue in the state to which the Lord called him and appointed him. This is the rule I give to all the churches. [18] For example, if a man was circumcised at the time Christ called him, he should remain circumcised. If he was not circumcised at the time of his call, he should not be circumcised. [19] For being circumcised or not being circumcised makes no difference at all. Keeping God's commands is what matters. [20] So I repeat, every man should remain as he was when he was called. [21] Were you a slave when God called you? Do not worry about it. But if you can get free, better take the opportunity!

[22] When a slave is called by the Lord, he becomes the Lord's free man. When a free man is called by the Lord, he becomes the slave of Christ. [23] The Lord bought you and paid for you. So do not let yourselves again become slaves of any man.

[24] So I say again, brethren, live your life with God in the same state you were in when God called you.

[25] Concerning those who are not married, I have no command from the Lord. But I will give you my opinion, and by the Lord's mercy I believe you can trust me. [26] I think that because of the

coming troubles it will be wise for single persons or married persons to remain as they are now. [27] My brother, if you have a wife, do not try to become free from her. If you are free now, do not try to find a wife. [28] But if you do marry, that is no sin. And if a girl marries, that is no sin. But those who are married have many troubles in the world. I would like to spare you those troubles.

[29] I mean to say, brothers, that the appointed time is becoming very short. From now on let those who have wives, live as though they had none. [30] Let those who weep, forget their tears. Let those who are happy, forget their joy. Let those who buy, live as though they had no goods. [31] Let those who have business in the world, live as though they had no business. For the present world order is about to pass away.

[32] I want you to be free from all worries about things of this world. The single man is eager for the Lord's work, and he tries to please only the Lord. [33] But a married man must worry about his affairs in this world, and he must try to please his wife. [34] His interests are divided.

A single girl or woman is anxious about the Lord's work. She tries to be holy in body and spirit. But the married woman is worried about the affairs of this world. She tries to please her husband.

[35] I say these things to help you, and not to rob you of your liberty. I am only trying to aid good order. I want only to be sure that you devote yourselves to the Lord and that your interests are not divided.

[36] But perhaps some man among you may think he is not acting right toward the girl he loves. His passions may be strong. He may feel that he ought to marry her. Then let him follow his heart and marry her. It is no sin. [37] Another man may make up his mind to keep his desire under control. He may feel no great passion. If he decides not to marry the girl he loves, he also is doing right. [38] So I say he who marries the girl he loves does right, but I think he who does not marry her is wiser.

³⁹ As for a wife, she is bound to her husband as long as he lives. If he dies, she is free to be married to anybody she likes, providing he loves the Lord. ⁴⁰ But in my judgment she will be happier if she remains as she is. And I think I have God's Spirit as I write.

8 Now I will answer the question about food offered to idols. You say: "We all know the truth about idols." Yes, we do, but knowledge makes a man swell with pride. It is love that builds up a man. ² A man may suppose that he knows all about something when he does not know as much as he needs to know. ³ Only when a man loves God does God approve of him.

⁴ This is true when we face the question about eating food offered to idols. We know that "an idol is not a real god." We know that "there is only one God." ⁵ The Gentiles, however, imagine that there are other gods in heaven or on earth. They have given names to many gods and lords. ⁶ But for us there is only one God, the Father. From Him came all things and we were made for Him. And for us there is only one Lord. He is Jesus Christ. By Him came all things. He gives us our life. ⁷ But not every one knows this. Some are new Christians who until recently have been used to idols. They still eat food as though it were really offered to a god. Then, their consciences, being weak, are injured.

⁸ You and I know that food does not bring us closer to God. We are no better men if we eat it, and no worse if we do not eat it. ⁹ But now take care that this right of yours does not cause weak people to be tempted. ¹⁰ Suppose somebody sees you attending a dinner in an idol's temple. This may tempt him to eat meat offered to idols. ¹¹ If the weak brother for whom Christ died goes against his conscience, he may be ruined by what you call your knowledge. ¹² So you may sin against your own brother by injuring his weak conscience. And that is sinning against Christ. ¹³ Suppose I find that my eating meat causes my brother

to fall. Then I will not eat meat for fear I may cause my brother to fall.

9   Am I not a free man? Yes, but I will give up all my rights, if only I can save others. Am I not an apostle? Have I not seen our Lord Jesus? Are not you Christians in Corinth the fruit of my work for the Lord? [2] You at least know I am an apostle even if some others do not believe it. You are yourselves the seal which proves that I am an apostle. [3] When people ask me why Barnabas and I do not live like the other apostles live this is my answer: We have the right to live as they live if we wish. [4] We have the right to ask the church to furnish our food and drink, do we not? Of course we have. [5] We have the right to take a Christian wife with us, have we not? Of course we have. The other apostles and the Lord's brothers and Peter all do that.

[6] Barnabas and I work at our trade for a living. We have a right to stop working, have we not? Of course we have. [7] What soldier, while he is in the army, must do other work to earn his expenses? Who plants a vineyard but cannot get any of the fruit? Who takes care of a flock and does not get any of the milk?

[8] I am not saying this only on human authority. The law of Moses says it also:

[9] "You shall not tie up the mouth of your ox while he
   is stamping out the grain with his feet." Let him eat.

Does God mean that to apply only to oxen? [10] Or does he mean to apply it to people as well? Yes, it applies to people. The man who plows has a right to his share of the crop. And the man who takes the grain from the straw has a right to his share.

[11] Barnabas and I have been sowing the good seed of the spirit among you. Does that not give us a right to ask you to provide something for us to live? Of course it does. [13] Those who work in the temple get their food from the temple. And those

who serve at the altar get their share of the food that is sacrificed.
¹⁴ Indeed the Lord himself commanded that those who preach
the Good News should get their living from it. ¹² If others have
a right to claim this of you, Barnabas and I have even more
right.

And yet we have never made use of this right. I will tell you
the reason. We would rather bear anything than put a block in
the way of the Good News of Christ. ¹⁵ Now you know why I
never accepted any help from you! And I am not asking you
for help now. In fact I would rather starve to death than let
people rob me of this one thing I have to boast about.

¹⁶ I dare not boast about preaching the Good News. I have no
free will about that. God compels me to do it. I am under His
command. Woe is me if I do not preach the Good News.

¹⁷ But if of my own free will I do more than God has commanded me to do, then He will reward me. ¹⁸ What am I doing
to earn this reward? Just this. I am refusing to accept pay from
you for preaching the Good News. I am refusing to take even
what God says I have a right to take.

¹⁹ I do not have to be any man's slave, and yet I have made
myself a slave to all men, so that I might win them to Christ.
²⁰ To the Jews I became like a Jew so that I might win Jews.
I am no longer under the law of the Jews, and yet I lived like
those who are under the law, so that I might win them to Christ.
²¹ I am now under another law: the law of Christ. And yet for
those who do not have that law, I have lived like a man without
the law so that I might win them to Christ. ²² To the weak I
became weak, so that I might win the weak. I have been all
things to all kinds of men. I have used every means to save at
least some of them. ²³ I do it for the sake of the Good News,
and for my hope of sharing some of its blessings.

²⁴ We know that in a race all the runners try to win, but only
one gets the prize. You must run to win the prize. ²⁵ When a
man enters the sports he practices self-control in every way. He
does this in order to win a crown of leaves which soon dry up

and die. But we are trying to win a crown that never is destroyed. [26] As for me I do not run without a clear purpose; I do not box like a man beating the air. [27] No! I beat my body; I keep it under my will. Because after I have preached to others, I would not want to fail to pass the test myself.

10 I do not want to fail as my brother Jews have failed. God gave them every chance. Remember that our fathers all marched under the cloud which God provided for them. And God brought all of them through the sea. [2] All of them were baptized into Moses. They were baptized by the cloud and by the sea. [3] All of them ate the food which God sent from heaven. [4] They all drank the water which God gave them. They drank from the Rock which God gave them and which traveled with them. That Rock was Christ. [5] Yet God was not pleased with most of them, and they were destroyed in the desert.

[6] This is a warning to us not to desire evil, as they did. [7] Do not worship idols as some of them did. As it is written,

> "The people sat down to eat and drink and then
> got up and danced."

[8] Let their fate be a warning to us not to fall into loose morals, as many of them did. Twenty-three thousand of them fell dead in one day. [9] Let us be warned not to tempt God as some of them did; and they were killed by snakes. [10] Let us be warned not to complain against God's commands as some of them did; and they were killed by the destroying angel. [11] All these things took place as a warning. They were written in our Holy Books to teach us not to do such things.

Today we stand close to the end of the world. [12] Let any one who thinks he can stand alone take care or he will fall. [13] But you will not be tempted more than other men are tempted. You can trust God. He will not let you be tempted beyond your strength. When you are tempted, God will provide the way of escape, so that you will be able to bear it.

¹⁴ But, my dear ones, keep entirely away from the worship of idols. ¹⁵ I am speaking to you as men of good sense, and I want you to think carefully while I explain the reason.

¹⁶ When we bless the cup, do we not share in the blood of Christ? When we break the bread do we not share in the body of Christ? ¹⁷ The very fact that we share one bread makes us all one body.

¹⁸ Look at what the Jews do. When they eat the meat that has been offered in the sacrifice, they share in the altar worship. ¹⁹ Now I do not claim that if we eat meat offered to idols, it makes us worship the idols. No, for an idol is nothing, and anything offered to the idol is nothing. ²⁰ And yet, when the heathen sacrifice they are really sacrificing to an evil spirit and not to God. And we do not wish to have anything to do with evil spirits. We cannot drink both the cup of the Lord and the cup of evil spirits. ²¹ So, I tell you we cannot share both the table of the Lord and the table of evil spirits. ²² We are not so strong that we dare to make God jealous. ²³ It is true that we are now free from the law, and yet not all things are good for us. We are free from the law and yet there are some things that do not build the church. ²⁴ Besides, in eating and in all other things, every one is to seek the good of his neighbor, and not just his own good. ²⁵ You may eat what is sold in the meat market without troubling your conscience. ²⁶ For

> "The earth is the Lord's, and everything in it is
> the Lord's."

²⁷ And if anybody who does not believe in Christ invites you to dinner and you wish to go, eat whatever is set before you without any question about your conscience. ²⁸ But if somebody says to you: "This has been offered to idols," then do not eat it. I say this not because of your own conscience. ²⁹ It is because you must not injure the conscience of the man who told you.

You may ask me why I allow my rights to be decided by another man's conscience. ³⁰ If I give thanks to God for the meat I eat, is it not all right for me to eat it? No, not if some weak brother condemns me for eating it. Here then is the rule to follow: ³¹ Whatever you do, and whatever you eat or drink, you must do it all to God's glory. ³² You must do nothing to tempt any man to do wrong, whether he is a Jew or a Greek or a member of the church of God. That is the rule I follow. I try to please all men in everything I do. I do not seek my own advantage. I seek only to save as many people as I can.

11 Follow my example, for I am following the example of Christ. ² I praise you because you always remember me in everything you do. You are holding fast to the teaching which I passed on to you. ³ Keep clearly in mind that Christ is the head of every man and God is the head of Christ. Also keep clearly in mind that the head of a woman is her husband.

⁴ If any man prays in public or preaches with his head covered, he brings shame upon his head. ⁵ But if a woman prays in public or preaches without covering her head she brings shame upon her head. She might as well have her head shaved! ⁶ So if a woman refuses to cover her head, then her hair should be cut like a man! But it would be a shame for a woman to have her hair cut or shaved off. No, the only way is for her to have her head covered. ⁷ A man does not cover his head, because a man is the image and glory of God, while a woman is the glory of man. ⁸ Woman was made from man, not man from woman. ⁹ Woman was created to help man, not man to help woman. ¹⁰ So as a sign of man's authority over her, a woman ought to cover her head, so the angels can see it. ¹¹ I realize, of course, that in God's sight the man is not independent of the woman, nor the woman of the man. ¹² For while woman was made from man, yet now man is born from woman. And really it is God who makes both men and women as well as everything else.

¹³ You decide this question for yourselves. Is it fitting for a woman to pray to God without covering her head? ¹⁴ Does it seem natural to you for a man to have long hair? ¹⁵ But if a woman

has long hair, is that not her glory? Her hair was given her to cover her head. [16] If any one wants to oppose my view of this question, my reply is: Neither I nor the churches follow any other custom.

[17] Now I shall write about a matter in which I cannot praise you. I hear that when you hold meetings you do more harm than good. [18] First of all I am told that in your church services you divide into parties. I am afraid this is partly true. [19] I am told that you think you must have groups so that the "best" people may be seen together. [20] And if what I hear is true about the way you meet in church, it certainly is not the Lord's supper that you eat. [21] I am told that each one gets his own supper and hurries to eat it. One man goes hungry while another gets drunk. [22] What is worse, you do this in the church! Have you not houses of your own to eat and drink in? You show no respect for the church of God. You make the poor members ashamed. [23] Shall I praise you for this? No!

I have told you what the Lord Himself told me about His last supper. On the night when He was betrayed, the Lord Jesus took bread. [24] And when He had given thanks He broke it, and said, "This is My body which I offer for you. Do this to remember Me." [25] In the same way He also took the cup after supper, and said: "This cup is the new agreement in My blood. As often as you drink this, do it to remember Me."

[26] Whenever you eat this bread or drink this cup you are telling others about the Lord's death until He comes. [27] So if any one eats the bread or drinks the cup in a way that is not worthy, he is sinning against the body and blood of the Lord. [28] Let a man examine himself before he eats of the bread and drinks the cup. [29] For any one who eats and drinks without seeing the body of Christ, eats and drinks judgment upon himself. [30] That is why many of you are weak, many are ill, and some have died. [31] If we always examine ourselves carefully, God will not need to pass judgment upon us. [32] Remember that when the

Lord judges us, he is correcting us, so that we may not be condemned along with the world.

[33] So, my brothers, when you meet together to eat, wait for one another. [34] If any one is too hungry to wait, let him eat at home. Then when you meet together you will not be condemned.

I will give you instructions about other things when I come.

12 Now, brothers, I wish to inform you about the gifts of the spirit. [2] You know that when you were not yet Christians you were led away to worship dumb idols, wherever your fancy took you. [3] We can always tell which is the true Spirit of God and which is not. For example, if any one says "Jesus be cursed," we know that the Spirit of God is not speaking. If any one says, "Jesus is Lord," we know that no one would say that unless the Holy Spirit helped him.

[4] People have many kinds of ability but all kinds came from the same Spirit. [5] People perform many kinds of service, but they have the same Lord. [6] God works through different men in different ways, but it is the same God who inspires them all. [7] Through each man the Spirit does what will bring about the greatest good to all. [8] To one man the Spirit gives words of wisdom, and to another man the Spirit gives words of knowledge. [9] The Spirit gives great faith to one man, and to another man He gives the power to heal diseases. [10] The Spirit gives one man the power to work miracles, and to another the power to preach, and to another the ability to understand different kinds of spirits. To one man the Spirit gives the power to speak in strange languages, and to another the ability to explain in plain words what these languages mean. [11] All these men are inspired by one and the same Spirit. To each man the Spirit gives that special gift which He wishes him to have.

[12] The human body is one, but it has many members. Though there are so many members, they are only one body. It is so with us and Christ. [13] For we are all baptized by one Spirit into

His one Body. Jews and Greeks, slaves and free men were all given to drink from the same cup and to receive the same Spirit.

[14] The body does not consist of one member only. It consists of many members. [15] Even if the foot should say: "I am not a hand, so I am not part of the body," it would still belong to the body. [16] If the ear should say, "I am not an eye, so I do not belong to the body," it would still be a part of the body. [17] If the whole body were an eye, how would it hear? If the whole body were an ear, how would it smell? [18] But as it is, God has arranged every organ of the body just where He wanted it. [19] If there were but one single organ, there would be no body. [20] There are many parts, but there is just one body.

[21] The eye cannot say to the hand, "I do not need you." The head cannot say to the feet: "I do not need you." [22] No, the very opposite is true. We cannot live without some parts of the body which seem to have little use. [23] And those parts of the body which we think have less honor, we dress very carefully. And those parts which we hide from view, we treat with the most reserve. [24] The parts of the body which we do not cover are not treated with so much reserve. When God put the body together, He gave the highest honor to some parts which we consider the least important. [25] The parts of the body do not fight against one another. Each member takes care of every other. [26] If one part suffers, all the others suffer with it. If one part of the body is honored, the whole body is full of joy.

[27] Now, all of you together are the body of Christ. Each of you is a member in Christ's body. [28] God has given each man his place in the church. First come the apostles. Second come the prophets. Third come the teachers. Then come those who work miracles. Then those who heal diseases. Then come those who help in the church. Then those who manage the church business. Then those who speak in strange languages. [29] Are they all apostles? Are they all prophets? Are they all teachers? Do they all work miracles? [30] Do they all heal diseases? Do they all

speak in strange languages? Can they all explain these languages in plain words? No, of course not.

³¹ And yet, it is right for us to desire the higher gifts. Now I will tell you the highest gift of all. It is love.

13 Suppose I speak in all the languages of men and of angels. If I have no love I am no more than a loud gong or a sounding cymbal.

² Suppose I have the gift of prophecy, and understand all secrets and possess all knowledge. Suppose I have enough faith to move mountains. If I have no love, I am good for nothing. ³ If I give away all I have to the poor, and even if I give my body to be burned, but have no love, it does me no good.

⁴ Love is patient. Love is kind. Love does not envy; love does not boast, it is not vain. ⁵ Love does not look down upon others; it is never rude. It does not insist upon having its own will. It does not get angry at little things; it does not nurse hurt feelings. ⁶ Love is not glad when others go wrong. It is glad when they do right. ⁷ Love stands true through every trouble, believes the best always, always hopes for the best, is always patient.

⁸ Love is the gift which never ends. The gift of prophecy will end. The gift of speaking in strange languages will end, knowledge will end. ⁹ Because we know only a little of the truth, and we prophesy only a little of the truth. ¹⁰ When we have perfect knowledge this small knowledge of ours will pass away. ¹¹ When I was a child, I spoke like a child, I thought like a child, I reasoned like a child. Now I am a man and have stopped acting like a child.

¹² As yet we cannot see the real world. We see only dark shapes of things as in a mirror. But in the next life we shall see everything clearly, face to face. Now I know only a little part, but then I shall understand it all, just as Christ now understands all about me.

¹³ Faith, hope, and love, these three last for ever. But the greatest of them all is love.

14 Aim first to have such love. Then, if you desire the other gifts of the Spirit, seek especially to preach. But do not try to speak in a strange language. [2] When any one speaks in strange languages, he does little to save other men, for he speaks not to men but to God. And no one understands the secrets he is telling except the Spirit of God. [3] But the man who preaches speaks words that build men up. He makes them strong, and gives them comfort. [4] The man who speaks strange languages builds himself up. The man who preaches builds the church up. [5] While I hope you will be able to speak in strange languages, I am more eager for you to preach. He who preaches is of greater use than he who speaks a strange language, unless some one explains it in plain words, so that the church may be built up.

[6] Brothers, if I come and speak to you in strange languages, do I help you? No, I do not help you unless I reveal some truth, or teach some knowledge, or preach.

[7] Unless clear notes are played on a flute or on a harp, will any one know what tune is played? [8] If the soldier who blows the horn does not sound a clear call to arms, who will prepare for battle? [9] It is the same with you if you speak in a strange language. Your words mean nothing to others. And if nobody knows what you have said, you are speaking into empty air. [10] There are many languages in the world. All of them have a meaning to somebody. [11] But if I do not understand the language which another man is speaking, I shall regard him as a stranger from a foreign land, and he will think the same of me.

[12] So this is what I tell you. If you are eager for gifts of the Spirit you should desire most those gifts which will build up the church. [13] If any one speaks in a strange language, let him pray that his words may be explained. [14] If I pray in a strange language, my spirit prays, but my mind helps nobody.

[15] What then am I to do? When I pray, I will pray with both my spirit and my mind. And when I sing praises, I will sing in words the people can understand. [16] If you praise God with your spirit in words which nobody understands, how can an ordinary

man say "Amen" to your praise? [17] You may give a beautiful prayer of thanks but you do not build the other man up. [18] I can speak strange languages more than any of you, and I thank God for this gift. [19] Yet in a church meeting, I would rather speak five plain words that would teach something to others than ten thousand words in a strange language.

[20] Brothers, do not be like children in your thinking. Be babies as far as evil is concerned, but in your thinking, be grown-up men. [21] In our law, it is written:

"I will speak to My people by the lips of strangers
    in a foreign language,
but My people will not listen to Me," says the
    Lord.

[22] Strange languages may act as a sign to win over those who do not yet believe. But they never do anything to build up those who have faith. Preaching, on the other hand, aims to help those who believe rather than those who do not believe. [23] Especially I warn you, never let people speak strange languages all at one time in your meetings. Some one from outside who does not believe, might enter, and he would think you were all mad. [24] But if he comes in when you are preaching, he may feel condemned for his sins. He may be called to account through your words. [25] The secrets in his heart may be laid bare. He may fall on his face and worship God, and declare that God is indeed with you.

[26] Here then is a good rule, brothers, when you hold meetings. One of you may sing a song of praise, another teach a lesson. Another may reveal the truth that God gave him. Another may speak in a strange language, and another may explain its meaning. Whatever you do in the service, always aim to build up the members of the church.

[27] If some of you want to speak in strange languages, do not allow more than two or at the most three to do so. Have each one speak in turn, and let some one explain it in plain words.

²⁸ If there is no one to explain it, tell them to keep silence in the church and speak their strange language within themselves to God.

²⁹ If some of you are inspired to preach, let two or three speak while the rest weigh what is said. ³⁰ If a person who is seated feels moved to tell what is revealed to him, the man who was preaching should stop. ³¹ You should all have a chance to speak and then every one will learn and be encouraged. ³² Those who are inspired to preach must keep their desire under control. ³³ God desires good order and peace in the church.

³⁴ As for the women, it is the custom in all the churches for them to keep quiet in church. They are not allowed to speak The law says that women should be under the rule of the men, and we follow that law. ³⁵ If they wish to ask about anything they should ask their husbands at home. We do not consider it proper for a woman to speak in church. ³⁶ Do any of you object to this custom? Well, I ask you, was it from Corinth that the word of God first came? Or are you the only people who heard it?

³⁷ If any man says he is filled with the Spirit, and if he thinks he is a prophet, he shall agree that what I have just written is the Lord's command. ³⁸ If he does not follow this custom, he should not be recognized.

³⁹ So my brothers, I say again that you should especially desire to preach. But if any one has an urge to speak in a strange language, allow him to do so. ⁴⁰ But do everything properly and in good order.

15 I want you to remember, brothers, the Good News which I preached to you. You received it. You now stand on it. ² And by it you are being saved, if you hold fast to it—unless you do not know what you really believe.

³ So I will tell you the most important truth which I received and passed on to you. It is this: Christ died for our sins as our Holy Writings said He would. ⁴ He was buried and was raised

on the third day, as our Holy Writings said He would be. [5] He appeared to Peter, then to the twelve. [6] Then He appeared to more than five hundred people at the same time. Most of those who saw Him are still alive, though some have since died. [7] Then He appeared to James, then to all the apostles. [8] Last of all He appeared to me, as to one who had been born too late. [9] I am the least of the apostles. I am not fit to be called an apostle, because I tried to destroy the church of God. [10] It is only by the grace of God that I am what I am. He did not give me His grace in vain, for I have worked harder than any of the other apostles. Yet, it was not I who worked, but the grace of God worked in me. [11] No matter who did the preaching, whether it was I or the other apostles, the truth that we all preached and that you believed was this:

[12] "Christ rose from the dead."

How then dare some of you say that nobody rises from the dead? [13] If nobody rises from the dead, then Christ did not rise. [14] If Christ did not rise, there is nothing in our preaching, and there is nothing in your faith. [15] In that case we are even giving false witness about God, because we declare that God raised Christ. Because if it be true that nobody ever rises from the dead, then God did not raise Christ. [16] If no one ever rises from the dead, then Christ did not rise. [17] If Christ did not rise, your faith is a sad mistake. You are still in your sins. [18] Those who died in Christ are lost. [19] If our hope in Christ goes no further than this life, we are of all men most to be pitied.

[20] But in fact Christ did rise from the dead. He was the first to rise of all those who have fallen asleep in death. [21] We die because the one man Adam sinned. We also rise from the dead because another Man, Christ, conquered death.

[22] In Adam all died. In Christ all shall be made alive. [23] Each one shall rise when his turn comes. Christ rose first. When He comes, those who belong to Him shall rise. [24] Then the end will come, and Christ will hand over His Kingdom to God the Father.

Christ will bring to an end every government, and authority, and power. [25] He must be king until He has put all His enemies under His feet. [26] The last enemy, death, will also be destroyed. [27] Our Holy Writings say:

"God put everything under Christ's feet."

It is clear, of course, that the word "everything" does not include God Himself. It was God who put everything under Christ's feet. [28] When at last everything is put under Christ, the Son will Himself be under the Father, Who gave it all to the Son. This will happen so that God may be everything to all men.

[29] If the dead did not rise, what would be the sense in people getting baptized for the dead? Why do they do it if the dead do not rise? [30] Yes, and why am I in danger every hour of my life? [31] Brothers, I am proud of what Jesus Christ our Lord has made of you. And I tell you that is why I face death every day. [32] I fought wild beasts in Ephesus. But from a human point of view, what good did it do, if the dead do not rise? If that were true, we might as well be like those who say,

"Let us eat and drink, for tomorrow we die."

[33] Do not be deceived. Thinking bad thoughts ruins good character. [34] To your shame I would say that some of you know nothing at all about the ways of God. Come back to your senses and sin no more.

[35] But some one will ask: "How are the dead raised? What kind of body will they have?" [36] Oh, foolish man to ask that question. What you sow in the ground never comes to life unless it dies first. You know that. [37] You do not sow the whole plant which will later grow up. You sow only a grain of wheat or some other seed. [38] God gives it the body which He intends it to have. He gives each kind of seed its own kind of body. [39] Not all flesh is the same. There is human flesh, and flesh of beasts, and flesh of birds and flesh of fish. [40] There are bodies of one kind in heaven, and bodies of another kind on earth. The bodies in

heaven have one kind of glory, and the bodies on earth have another kind of glory. ⁴¹ There is one glory of the sun, another of the moon, and another of the stars. And each star is different from every other in glory.

⁴² So also people are very different after they rise from the dead. The dead body is like seed which is sown in the earth and which dies. The new body that is raised from the dead body, never dies again. ⁴³ The dead body is sown in the earth to decay, but the new body is raised to glory. When it is sown it is weak; when it is raised it has great power. ⁴⁴ When it is sown it is a physical body. When it is raised it is a spirit body. Just as there is a physical body, so there is a spirit body. ⁴⁵ This is why it is written:

"The first Adam became a living being."

The last "Adam" who is Christ, became a Spirit. He gives life to others.

⁴⁶ The physical life comes first, not the living spirit. The living spirit comes later. ⁴⁷ The first man came from the earth. He was made of dust. The second Man was from heaven. ⁴⁸ Those who belong to the earth are like the first man who was made of dust. Those who belong to heaven are like the Man from heaven. ⁴⁹ Now we are like the man of dust, but then we shall be like the Man from heaven. ⁵⁰ I tell you, brothers, that flesh and blood cannot live in the kingdom of God. That which dies cannot possess that which never dies.

⁵¹ Listen now while I tell you a secret. Not all of us shall fall asleep in death. But we shall all be changed. ⁵² In a moment, quicker than the eye can wink, we shall be changed when the angel blows the last horn. The horn shall sound and the dead shall rise, never to die again. We shall all be entirely different. ⁵³ The nature that can be destroyed must change into a nature that cannot be destroyed. The nature that dies must change into a nature that never dies. ⁵⁴ That which can be destroyed shall change into that which cannot be destroyed. That which dies

shall change to that which never dies. Then shall come true these words:

⁵⁵ "He shall win the victory over death.

O death, where is thy victory?

O death, where is thy power to hurt us?"

⁵⁶ Sin gave death its power to hurt. And the law gave sin its power. ⁵⁷ But thank God, He sent our Lord Jesus Christ to give us the victory.

⁵⁸ Therefore, dear brothers, stand firm and let nothing move you. Keep busy all the time with the work of the Lord. You may be sure that your labor for the Lord will bear fruit.

16 Now let me write about collecting money for God's people. Do it the way I directed the churches in Galatia to do it. ² Every week on the first day, each one of you is to take something from his earnings, and save it until I come. Then the money will not need to be collected after I arrive. ³ Then choose some men to bear the gift. Write a letter giving them this authority, and I will send them on with it to Jerusalem. ⁴ If it seems wise, I will go to Jerusalem also and take them with me.

⁵ I plan first to pass through Macedonia, and from Macedonia I will come down to visit you. ⁶ Perhaps I will stay with you for some time, and I may spend the winter with you. Then you may see me on my way wherever I may decide to go. ⁷ When I come, I want to have more than a short look at you. I should like to have a good long visit with you if the Lord permits.

⁸ But I am staying here in Ephesus until Pentecost. ⁹ The door is wide open here for me to get good results. But I have many enemies.

¹⁰ When Timothy gets to Corinth, make him feel at home among you. He is doing the Lord's work just as I am. ¹¹ Do not look down upon him. Send him back to me with his heart at peace. I shall be expecting him to return with the other brothers. ¹² I urged our brother Apollos to go with these other brothers

to visit you, but it was not God's will for him to go. He will come later when he has another opportunity.

[13] Be on your guard, stand firm in your faith. Be brave. Be strong. [14] Let all that you do be done with love.

[15] You remember, brothers, that Stephanas and his family were the first in Greece to become Christians. They have given their time and strength to the service of God's people. [16] I urge you to follow such men and all our fellow workers who labor for the Lord.

[17] I am so glad that Stephanas and Fortunatus and Achaicus came to Ephesus to see me. They made up for your not being here. [18] They encouraged my spirit as they had always encouraged yours. Show all honor to such men.

[19] The churches in Asia send you their best wishes. Aquila and Prisca and the church which meets in their house send their warm greetings in the Lord. [20] All the brothers send greetings. Greet one another with a holy kiss.

[21] And now I, Paul, am writing this last sentence with my own hand. [22] If any one has no love for the Lord, let a curse be on him.

Come Lord Jesus!

[23] The grace of the Lord Jesus be with you. [24] My love goes out to all of you who are in Christ Jesus. Amen.

Paul
Sosthenes

PAUL'S SECOND LETTER
TO THE CHRISTIANS IN CORINTH

From Ephesus, Asia

From: *Paul, whom God appointed as an apostle of Christ Jesus*

To: *The Church of God in Corinth*

1 Our brother Timothy joins me in writing this letter. We are writing to you and to all the people of God in Greece.

² May God our Father and the Lord Jesus Christ give you grace and peace. ³ Praise be to God the Father of our Lord Jesus Christ. He is our Father who has shown us mercy. He is our God who has given us comfort. ⁴ He has comforted us in our sufferings. And we are comforting others who are suffering just as God does us.

⁵ I, myself, have had a very large share in Christ's suffering. But Christ has also given me a very large share of His comfort. ⁶ I have suffered so that you, too, might be comforted and saved. Be patient when you suffer as I am patient. Then I shall be comforted in my sorrow and I know God will also comfort you. ⁷ My hope for you is never shaken. I know that you have suffered just as I have. I know also that you will be comforted just as I am.

⁸ I want to tell you, brothers, how I have been suffering here in Asia. I was crushed far beyond what I could stand, and I thought I was going to die. ⁹ I thought this was my death sentence. But that terrible experience made me depend, not on myself, but entirely on God who can raise the dead. ¹⁰ God has delivered me from death. And He will deliver me the next time. I have put my hope in Him to save me always. ¹¹ Help me with your prayers. God will answer your prayers, and many a soul will thank Him for the blessing He has granted me.

¹² In my dealings with the world and with you I have been perfectly honest and holy in God's sight. My conscience is clear about that. Of that indeed I am proud. I have never put my trust in the world's wisdom but only in God's grace.

¹³ Now I am going to write some very plain things which mean just what they say. I hope you will understand them clearly. ¹⁴ I think you do partly understand already. I am eager to be proud of all of you, when the Lord Jesus comes, and I want you to be proud of me.

¹⁵ The first thing I want to tell you plainly is why I did not visit you. I had fully intended to visit you. I wanted very much to pay you two visits, and I hoped that those two visits would give you double pleasure. ¹⁶ I wanted to visit you on the way up to Macedonia, and again on the way back from Macedonia. I had planned that you should then send me on my way to Judea.

¹⁷ Why, then, do you suppose I decided not to come? Do you imagine I am the kind of man who cannot make up his mind? Or do you imagine I am like men of the world who say "Yes" one moment and break their word the next? You know I am not like that. ¹⁸ God knows that my words to you have never left you doubting whether I meant "Yes" or "No." ¹⁹ Silvanus and Timothy and I preached to you that Jesus Christ is the Son of God. We never said "Yes" and then changed to "No" about Christ. We always said "Yes." ²⁰ We told you that every promise God ever made finds its "Yes" in Christ. In Him every promise comes true. When men talk about God we cry: "Amen. Thank God for Christ."

²¹ It was God who made our faith and your faith solid in Christ. He appointed us. ²² He poured His Holy Spirit into our hearts. The Holy Spirit was the seal which He put upon all of us. That was the proof that made us sure.

²³ "Then why," you ask, "did you not come to Corinth?" I will tell you the straight truth. It was to spare you more pain. I call God to witness that this was the real reason. ²⁴ I did not

want to issue hard commands again as I did in my other visit. I wanted only to work to give you joy. For your faith is firm enough.

2 So I made up my mind that I would not pay you another visit if it meant causing you pain. [2] If I were to give you pain I would be hurting the very friends who give me the greatest joy.

[3] That is why I wrote that other letter to you. I wrote it so that when I came I might not be hurt by those who should give me joy. I felt sure that you would be happy only if I were happy. [4] While I was writing to you I was troubled and suffering and in tears. I did not write to hurt your feelings. I only wanted you to know how much I loved you.

[5] That man who was living in sin among you caused pain not only to me, but more or less to you also. I say kindly that I wish it had pained you more. [6] The majority of you did condemn him as I told you to do. That was enough punishment. [7] Now I hope you will forgive and comfort him. If you do not forgive him he may die of shame and sorrow. [8] So I beg you to tell him that you love him again.

[9] I wrote those hard demands in the letter to test you. I wanted to find out whether you would obey me perfectly. You did! [10] Now if you forgive him, I forgive him too. In the presence of Christ I have forgiven that man for your sakes. [11] We must keep Satan from gaining a victory. We all know what Satan aims to do.

[12] I came to Troas, and found the door wide open for me to preach the Good News of Christ. [13] But my mind could not rest because I did not find my brother Titus there. So I said "Goodbye" and came on here to Macedonia.

[14] Thank God, Who is giving us victory after victory by the help of Christ. We are spreading the knowledge of Him like perfume everywhere. [15] We are perfume as from Christ to God, to those who are saved. But we are quite a different smell to those who are lost. [16] To one we are the perfume of life; to

another we are the smell of death. Who is worthy to be trusted with such a message!

¹⁷ Many are selling God's word for their own gain. But we are not. We have but a single purpose. We were chosen and sent by God. We remember that His eye is on us, and that Christ is in us as we speak.

3 I hope you are not saying: "Paul is beginning to praise himself." Oh, no! You and I do not need to write letters to one another to prove our character. Some people need such letters, but you and I do not need them. ² Because you yourselves are my letters of credit. I wrote them in your hearts, open for all men to read and understand. ³ Your lives show that you are letters sent from Christ and carried by me. These letters were not written with ink. They were written with the Spirit of the living God. They were not written on tables of stone, but on your human hearts.

⁴ Our confidence is all in God through Christ. ⁵ We know we are not fit to claim any credit for ourselves. It is God alone Who makes us fit to be His servants. ⁶ He alone gives us strength to offer to men His new agreement with them. This new agreement is not written down on stone like the laws of Moses. It was written by the Spirit of God. You know that the written law brought us death, but the Spirit gives us life.

⁷ The law of Moses that brought death was cut in stone. It came shining with terrible glory. The Jews could not look on the face of Moses even after that terrible light began to fade away. ⁸ Why, I ask, should not the work of the Holy Spirit come with even greater glory? ⁹ Great glory was shining when the law came that brought death. So the way to become right with God should come with a far more brilliant light. ¹⁰ The law of Moses came with a very bright light. But now it has no glory at all for us, compared to the glory of the new bond that brings us life. ¹¹ That brilliant light which came with the law of Moses soon faded

away. The new light of Christ is much more splendid for it will never fade away.

¹² Our hope in Christ makes us speak out with no fear. ¹³ I do not act as Moses did when he covered his face with a veil. He was afraid that the Jews might be killed if they saw his fading glory. ¹⁴ The truth is, it was their minds which were covered with a veil. Even today when the Jews read the old bond which God gave Moses, their minds are behind a veil. Only Christ can lift that veil off their minds. ¹⁵ So to this day the veil remains on their minds whenever the law of Moses is read to them. ¹⁶ But whenever any man turns to the Lord, the veil is removed and he can see the truth.

¹⁷ The Spirit which we have is the Lord Himself in us. When the Spirit of the Lord comes in, our minds are set free. ¹⁸ Then the veil is taken from our faces. We look straight at the glory of God. We are changed and become like Him. We pass from one glory to another. This change is made by the Lord who is the Spirit working in us.

4 It is only by the mercy of God that I am in this work. That is why I never lose heart. ² And I will not do a thing that is not perfectly straight and honest. I refuse to use tricks to deceive people. I will not change the word of God to please anybody. I tell the plain truth to everybody. I want men's consciences also to approve my work in the sight of God. ³ If our Good News is ever veiled, it is veiled only to those who are lost. ⁴ The god of this world has blinded the minds of those who do not believe. This keeps them from seeing the light of the Good News. They cannot see the glory of Christ who is just like God. ⁵ I preach about the Lord Jesus Christ, not about myself. I am nothing but a slave working for Jesus and for you. ⁶ God said, "Let light shine where it is dark." And it is God Who shines in our hearts, where it was dark. He makes us able to see and know the light and glory of God in the face of Christ.

⁷ But He gives us this treasure in a clay vessel—that is what

our bodies are—clay vessels. He has made my body weak so that I will remember that the divine power belongs to God and not to me.

⁸ I am suffering in every way, but I am not crushed. I have many difficulties, but I have not lost hope. ⁹ I am ill treated, but God has not left me. I am struck down, but I am not killed. ¹⁰ I always carry marks on my body to remind me of the death of Jesus. This is how Jesus makes His life seen in my body.

¹¹ Every day of my life I face death for the sake of Jesus. In this way Jesus can reveal Himself through my dying flesh. ¹² Death works in me so that Christ can pour His life into you. ¹³ I have the same kind of faith as the one who wrote,

> "I believed, and so I spoke."

Well, that expresses my faith and my spirit. I believe and so I dare speak out. ¹⁴ For I know that God, who raised the Lord Jesus from death, will also raise me up from death with Jesus and bring me into His presence. And He will bring you, too. ¹⁵ All I do is done for your sakes. As God gives His grace to more and more people like you, I shall have more and more reason to thank and praise Him.

¹⁶ So I never lose heart. My outside body is wasting away, but inside my spirit gets new strength every day. ¹⁷ Our little sufferings in this world do not last long. They are preparing us for a glory that will last for ever. Compared to that glory our sufferings are nothing. ¹⁸ We do not look at the things which people can see. We are looking at the things they cannot see. The things they see soon pass away. The things they do not see will last for ever.

5 Our bodies are like tents in which we live for a while. We know that when the tents are destroyed, we shall have a house from God. That house was not built with hands. It is in heaven and it will last for ever. ² Here in these tents we sigh for our home in heaven. ³ When we enter that home in heaven we shall

not be without clothes. Indeed we shall be far better clothed than we are now. ⁴ While I stay in this tent on earth I sigh and am anxious to go. This is not because I want to be without clothes but because I want better clothes than these. I am eager for my dying body to be exchanged for a body that will live for ever. ⁵ It is God who is preparing you and me for this change. He has given us the Holy Spirit to make us sure of the glory which is to come.

⁶ This is why I am not afraid to die. I know that staying in this body is only keeping me from the Lord. ⁷ I cannot see clearly here and I have to walk by faith. ⁸ So I look upon death without any fear. In fact, I would rather leave this body and be at home with the Lord. ⁹ But whether I remain here on earth or go home to Him, I aim always to please Him. ¹⁰ Some day we must all appear before the judgment seat of Christ. Each of us will then receive good or evil depending upon the life he has lived in the body.

¹¹ It is because men must fear the judgment of God that I try to persuade people to be saved. God knows exactly what kind of man I am. I hope that down in your hearts you know too. ¹² I do not think I need to write any praise of my work to you. And yet I do want you to have cause to be proud of me. I want you to be able to answer those people who judge a man by the office he holds, not by what is in his heart. ¹³ If some people think I am acting like a mad man, I do it for God's sake. But you know that I am acting in my right mind. I want only to help you.

¹⁴ The love of Christ controls us. We know that Christ died for all of us. So our old self died with Him. He meant that those who are saved by His death should no longer live for themselves. ¹⁵ He meant that they should live for Him who died for them and rose from the dead.

¹⁶ We once looked upon Christ the way people of the world do, but we do so no longer. And so of course we do not look upon any man the way those other people do. ¹⁷ If a man is in

Christ, he is created new. The man that he was has passed away, and, behold, a new man has been created!

[18] It was God who did all this. He sent Christ to make everything right between God and us. Then He called us to go and bring other men back to Him. [19] God in Christ came into the world to bring men back to Him. If they accept His offer He does not count their sins against them any longer.

God has trusted me to tell men about His offer to forgive and accept them. [20] Christ is sending me from place to place to carry this message. Through my voice, God is calling you all. Speaking for Christ, I say to every man: "Turn from your sins and get right with God." [21] Christ has opened the way. He knew no sin, but He died for our sins, so that now we may be counted right in the sight of God.

6 That is God's offer which we workers for God brought to you. You accepted it. Now we appeal to you not to lose what God gave you by His grace. [2] God said:

"When I was ready to accept you, I listened to you;
and when I chose to save you, I came to your help."

Behold, this is the time He is ready to accept you. This is the day when He chooses to save you.

[3] I have never put a thing in the way of men that would keep them from God. I want nobody to be able to find fault with my service. [4] For I am God's servant and I want Him to be satisfied with all I do. I have had to go through sufferings, difficulties, terrible troubles, [5] beatings, prisons, angry crowds, hard labor, nights without sleep, and hunger. [6] I have lived a pure life. I have been patient and kind, and my love has been real. God has blessed me with His Holy Spirit, and with knowledge, and with His power. [7] I have told the truth: I have lived a straight life. This has been my only weapon against enemies on my right and on my left. [8] I have known honor and suffered shame. I have faced good reports and bad reports. I have been charged

with deceiving when I spoke only the truth. ⁹ Men have called me an unknown nobody when I was well known. They said I was dying, but I am still alive. They punished me, but they have not yet killed me. ¹⁰ I am full of sorrow and yet full of joy. I am very poor yet I am making many rich. I have nothing yet I possess everything.

¹¹ Oh, my brothers in Corinth, I have opened my heart and told you everything that I feel. ¹² Oh, brothers, I have gone all the way in my love for you, yet you seem to be holding back in your love of me.

¹³ I am speaking to you as to children. Open your hearts all the way to me. That will pay me back for all I have done for you.

¹⁴ Now, brothers, do not get tied up with men who refuse to accept Christ. How can good and evil be fellow workers? How can light and darkness be in the same place at the same time? ¹⁵ How can Christ and Belial agree? What can the man who believes in Christ have in common with the man who does not believe? ¹⁶ What kind of contract could the temple of God sign with idols? We are the temple of the living God. For God Himself said:

> "I will live in them; I will walk with them.
> I will be their God; they shall be My people."

¹⁷ God also says:

> "Come out from among those who do wrong;
> be separated from them," says the Lord.

> "Touch nothing that is not clean
> then I will welcome you; ¹⁸ I will be your Father.
> You shall be My sons and daughters,"
> says the Lord who is mighty over all.

7   These are the promises we have received, dear brothers. So let us wash ourselves clean from everything that is not pure for

the body or for the spirit. Let us aim to be perfectly holy in the fear of God.

² And oh, my dear friends, take me into your hearts. I have never wronged any of you, never harmed any of you, never taken advantage of any of you. You know that! ³ In saying this I am not blaming you in the least. Oh no, it is because you are already in my heart, as I told you before. We must live together; and we must die together. ⁴ I believe in you with all my heart. I am proud of you. You are my greatest comfort. Because of you I am filled with joy even in my sufferings.

⁵ Oh, how I suffered in Macedonia! When I reached there my poor body had no peace. I met with trouble on every side. Outside of me there was fighting and inside there was fear. ⁶ But God comes to help those whose hearts are heavy. He comforted me by Titus' arrival. ⁷ His coming was a great relief to me. The news of the kind welcome you gave him made me very happy. He told me how you longed to see me. He told me how sorry you were because of what had happened. When he told me how you loved me and believed in me, I was happiest of all. ⁸ I knew how my former letter must have hurt you. I had often wished that I had never sent it. But now I do not regret that letter any longer. I see that it hurt you only for a while. ⁹ I am happy now not because you were made sorry but because your sorrow led to a change of heart. You became sorry as God wanted you to become. To my great joy not one of you left the church because of what I said. ¹⁰ The grief which God wants men to feel produces a change of heart. Then God can save them and they need have no more regret. But grief without God kills men. ¹¹ See what God has done for you through the grief my letter caused you! How serious it made you! How eager it made you to clear yourselves! How hurt and angry and alarmed you were at those who did wrong! How you longed for me to come! How anxious you were to right the wrong! How you punished the man who sinned! In every way you proved that you were not to blame for his sin.

[12] I did not write that letter on account of the man who sinned. And I did not write it on account of the man whom he wronged. I wrote it to prove to you in the sight of God how earnest your love for me was. [13] You met the test and I am very happy. I am especially happy because Titus was so full of joy about you. All his doubts about you are gone. [14] Many times I had told Titus how proud I was of you, and now you have proved that I was not mistaken. Everything I had said about you proved to be true. I had boasted about you, and you lived up to my boasting. [15] Titus says that his heart goes out to you as he remembers how you obeyed him. He says that you received him with holy fear and trembling, and he loves you. [16] How glad I am that I can have such perfect confidence in you.

8 Now brothers, we want to tell you about God's grace to the churches here in Macedonia. [2] They have had a severe testing and have suffered greatly. Yet they are full of joy. They were very poor. But their own need made them even more eager to send help to Jerusalem. [3] We can witness that they gave all they could afford and more than they could afford. They gave it of their own free will. [4] In fact they begged us for the favor of letting them have a part in the relief of God's people in Jerusalem. [5] They did far more than we had ever expected. They began by giving themselves to the Lord. Then they promised God that they would help us carry out His will.

[6] When Titus visited you the other time he began to gather your gifts for the people of God in Jerusalem. Now he is bringing you this letter. So we urged him to finish gathering these gifts of loving kindness which you began to give last year. [7] You are so excellent in every way—in your faith and speech and knowledge and eager desire to do right and in your love for us. Be first also in this work of loving kindness.

[8] I do not write this at all as a command. But I have seen how eager the other churches are to help, and I knew you also would be eager to show how real your love is. [9] You know how much

our Lord Jesus Christ loved you and how much He gave for you. Though He was rich, yet for your sake He became poor so that you might become rich.

10 A year ago you were the first to think of helping the Christians in Jerusalem and you were the first to give anything to them. So here is what I suggest. 11 It will be fine now for you to complete what you started to do then. This will show the other churches that you are as much in favor of it now as you were when you started it last year. Give what you can. 12 If a man is willing to give what he can, God accepts that. God judges a man's giving by what he has, and does not expect him to give if he is not able.

13 I do not mean to let other churches get off easily while you carry the burden. 14 No, I mean that every person should give according to his ability to give. You are prospering now while the churches in Macedonia are in want. So you are able to supply what they could not give. Some other time they may have plenty and you may have need of help. Then they will be able to supply what you lack. Thus you will help one another. 15 It is written in the Holy Writings:

"He who gathered much had nothing over,
and he who gathered little had enough."

16 I thank God for putting in the heart of Titus so much loving concern for you. 17 We suggested to Titus that he take this letter to you. He not only agreed to go, but he was very eager to go. He said he would have gone even if we had not asked him.

18 With Titus we are sending another brother who is well known among the churches for his preaching of the Good News. 19 He was chosen by the people of God to travel with us in this work. The reason we are collecting this aid for the Christians of Jerusalem is because it brings glory to God. It also shows that the people of God are willing to help each other.

20 We are careful and honest in managing these gifts of love, and we do not want even one person to doubt it. 21 We want to

do right, not only in God's sight, but also in the sight of all men. ²² With these two men we are sending to you still a third brother. We have often put him to the test and have found him interested in all good things. He is now very eager to go along to visit you because he has such confidence in you.

²³ Titus is my very close friend and companion in my work for you. The other two brothers represent the churches and they are both a credit to the cause of Christ. ²⁴ So prove to them and to the churches which they represent that our boasting about your love is all true.

9 I know very well that I do not need to urge you to give to God's people. ² I know how ready you are to do this. I have been boasting about you to all the people of Macedonia. I told them that you Christians in Greece have been ready to give these gifts since last year. Your enthusiasm has stirred up most of them to give. ³ I send these men now just to make sure that our boasting does not turn out to be empty. We want to be sure that you are still ready to help as I told the people you would be. ⁴ It would be just too bad if some men from Macedonia came along with us when we visit you and found that you were not ready. We would feel ashamed and so would you, after all our praise of you. ⁵ So I thought I ought to send these brothers on ahead of me. They can help in collecting the gift which you promised and it will be all ready when I come. This way it will not be a forced payment, but a willing gift. ⁶ You remember the saying:

> "He who sows little will gather a little harvest;
> he who sows much will gather a big harvest."

⁷ That is true. Yet each person must make up his own mind what he will give. He must not be pushed or compelled to give. God loves the man who is happy when he gives. ⁸ But do not let fear for the future prevent you from being generous. God is able to bless you with more than you need. He will give you so

much that you will always be able to give to every good cause.
⁹ It is written:

> "God scatters with a full hand.
> He gives to the poor.
> His kindness will last forever."

¹⁰ God supplies seed for the farmer to sow and bread for him
to eat. He will also supply you with all the seed you need to
sow deeds of kindness. He will give you a big harvest of kind
deeds. ¹¹ God will make you rich in all things: rich enough for
you to be a great blessing to the poor. Your generous gift
through me will make many people thank God for you. ¹² Generous giving works that way. You will do more than take care
of the needs of God's people in Jerusalem; you will also produce
an outpouring of praises to God. ¹³ And more than that, your
giving will prove that your religion is real. If you make a generous
gift to them and to others, every one will thank God and say:
"These Christians not only believe in Christ; they also practice
what they believe." ¹⁴ They will love you, long to see you, and
pray for you, because you have so much of God's grace in your
hearts. ¹⁵ I thank God that He has given you far more than
words can describe.

10 I, Paul, am now appealing to you with the humble gentle
spirit of Christ. Some people say that I use strong language in
my letters when I am away from you, but am humble when face
to face with you. ² Well, I beg you that when I come I may not
be forced to use strong language. I am afraid I shall have to be
hard on some of you. I hear that some one is saying that we
follow the customs of the world. He is not telling the truth.
³ We live in the world but we do not follow its customs. We
do not fight as men of this world fight. ⁴ The weapons we use
are not the weapons this world uses. Our weapons have the
power of God to destroy the defenses of evil. We destroy arguments. ⁵ We destroy every mountain of pride that stands in the

way of the knowledge of God. We capture every thought and make it obey Christ. ⁶ And we are ready to punish any one who claims to follow Christ but does not obey Him.

⁷ Look at what is going on in Corinth before your very eyes. That man is telling you that he was chosen by Christ. Remind him that I, too, was chosen by Christ. ⁸ Perhaps I seem to boast too much about the authority God gave me. If I do so it is to build you up and never to destroy you. ⁹ That man is not telling you the truth when he says I am trying to make you afraid with my letters. ¹⁰ I hear that some are saying: "Paul's letters sound big and strong, but he is a weak little thing and his speeches are no good." Tell those people this: ¹¹ When I come to Corinth my actions will be just as strong as my letters are while I am away.

¹² I would not even try to compare myself to that man who is saying such big things about himself! He measures himself by his own standards and he is not showing good sense.

¹³ I shall not boast more than I should. I measure myself by the job which God gave me to do. He sent me to preach His Good News to you and I did it. ¹⁴ I was the first to come to you in Corinth with the Good News of Christ.

I never go beyond the authority which God gave me. ¹⁵ I never take credit for work other men have done. My hope is that, as your faith increases, you will help us ¹⁶ extend the Good News also in lands beyond Greece. I do not want to boast about work done in any other man's field.

¹⁷ "Let him who boasts, boast of the Lord."

¹⁸ For God does not approve of the man who praises himself. It is the man whom the Lord praises who is accepted.

11   And now I wish you would let me say some foolish things. Please do. ² I am jealous of you just as God is jealous of you. For I have promised you in marriage to Christ. I want to present you to Him pure like a bride for her husband. ³ The serpent de-

ceived Eve with his smart lies. I am afraid that same serpent may lead your thoughts away from the true and holy love of Christ. ⁴ For that other man in Corinth is preaching a different Jesus from the Jesus we preached. From him you get a wholly different spirit from ours. You hear a different "Good News" from the one we preached. And why do you allow him to do this without any protest! He says he is an "apostle." ⁵ I do not believe I am in a lower class than these wonderful "apostles." ⁶ I know I cannot make a good speech, but I do have knowledge. I think that is plain to you all.

⁷ Did I lose your respect because I did not charge you anything when I preached God's message to you? I took a humble place so that you might take a high place. Was that a sin? ⁸ I let the other churches pay for my support so that I could work for you. ⁹ I was in real want when I was with you, yet I never asked you for a thing. The brothers who came from Macedonia supplied what I needed. That is how I kept from being a burden to you in any way. And I am going to keep from burdening you. ¹⁰ By all the truth of Christ that is in me, this boast shall not be taken from me by any man in Greece! ¹¹ And why do I say this? Is it because I do not love you? God knows that I do love you. ¹² But I am going to keep on living without your support. I am doing this in order to cut the ground from under those "apostles" who boast that they work "on the same terms" as we work. ¹³ They are false "apostles" deceiving you, pretending to be apostles of Christ. ¹⁴ Do not wonder at this, for even Satan dresses himself up to look like an angel of light. ¹⁵ So it is not strange if Satan's servants dress themselves up to look like servants of right. In the end they will get what they deserve.

¹⁶ As I said before, I hope you will not think I am foolish. But even if you do think so, accept me as a fool, and let me boast a little. ¹⁷ I am not writing this with the Lord's authority. I will boast like that foolish man among you in Corinth, who talks about himself so much. ¹⁸ Since other people are boasting

about what they own or do, why can't I boast? [19] You seem pleased to bear with a fool. You are so wise, [20] yet you will let a man make slaves of you, live on you, take advantage of you, put on airs, strike you in the face. [21] I am ashamed to say that I am too weak to act as he acts. But if any one insists on boasting about himself I will boast like a fool too.

> [22] Are they Hebrews? So am I.
> Are they sons of Israel? So am I.
> Are they sons of Abraham? So am I.

[23] Are they ministers of Christ? I am a better one. (What a mad fool I am to boast like this!) I have worked harder than he has. I have been in prison more times than he has. I have been beaten so many times that I cannot count them. I have often been nearly dead. [24] Five different times the Jews gave me thirty-nine strokes with the whip. [25] Three times I was beaten with rods; once I was stoned; three times I was in shipwrecks. I spent a night and a day in the sea. [26] I have taken many journeys. I have been in danger from rivers. I have been in danger from robbers. I have often been in danger from my own people and in danger from the Gentiles. I have been in danger in cities, in deserts, and in the sea. I have been in danger from false brothers. [27] I have gone through hard labor and great suffering. I have had many nights with no sleep. I have been through hunger and thirst, often with no food at all. I have been cold and without clothes. [28] In addition to all these things I have had the work and worry of the churches on my mind every day. [29] If any one is weak, I am weak with him. When any one leads another into sin, I burn with anger about it. [30-33] At Damascus, the governor under King Aretus put guards around the city and ordered them to seize me. But I was let down in a basket through a window in the wall, and I escaped from him.

If I boast I must boast about these things that show how weak I am. God the Father of the Lord Jesus Christ knows that I have not lied about them. (Blessed be His name for ever.)

12 I want to boast about one more thing, though I realize there is nothing to gain by it. I will tell about visions and what the Lord has revealed to me. ² I know a Christ-filled man who was caught up to the third heaven fourteen years ago. Whether this man was in his body or out of his body I do not know. God knows. ³ But I do know that this man was caught up to paradise. (I do not know whether he was in his body or out of his body. Only God knows.) ⁴ There he heard things which cannot be told, things which no man dare speak. ⁵ I will boast about that man. About myself I will boast only that I am weak. ⁶ If I wished to boast, I would not be a fool for I would be telling the truth. But I am not going to do it. I do not want any one to think more of me than he sees in my life and hears from me about Christ.

⁷ To keep me from being too full of joy about the wonders which Christ revealed to me, he has let me suffer with a "thorn in the flesh." A servant of Satan troubles me and keeps me from being too happy. ⁸ Three times I asked the Lord to save me from this trouble. But God said to me: ⁹ "My grace is enough for you. When you are weak then My power is made perfect." So I will boast about being weak, for then the power of Christ can come upon me. ¹⁰ For the sake of Christ, I am content to be weak, to be called evil names, to suffer, to be ill-treated, to face disasters. For when I am weak, then I find I am strong.

¹¹ What a fool I have been to boast like this! But you forced me to do it. You are the ones who ought to have been boasting about me. For in not one respect am I below those "wonderful apostles," even though they say I am nothing. ¹² You saw in me all the signs of a true apostle when I was with you. You saw how patient I was. You saw the signs and wonders and mighty works which God did through me. ¹³ In what way did I favor you less than other churches? Was it that I did not ask you to pay for my living? Forgive me if I wronged you in that.

¹⁴ I am about ready now to pay you my third visit. But again I am not going to let you pay my expenses. I do not want your money; I want you. Children are not expected to save money for

their parents; parents do that for their children. [15] I shall be happy to spend all I have and all I am for your sakes. Are you going to love me less, because I love you more? [16] I suppose that the false leader who is among you will say: "No, Paul did not take any pay when he was with you, but that was just his smart trick to deceive you." [17] You know that is not true. Did I take advantage of you when I sent those men to you with my letters? [18] I asked Titus to go to Corinth with another brother. Did Titus take any money from you for himself? Did not Titus act the same as I did and follow the same plan?

[19] I am afraid you think that I have been trying to defend myself. No. I am not on trial. But I have said this, beloved, in the sight of God. I have said it in Christ, only for your sakes, to build you up. [20] I am so afraid I may come to Corinth and not find you as I wish you to be. If you are doing wrong, you will certainly not find me the way you wish me to be. I am so afraid I may find you quarreling and jealous. I am afraid I shall find you talking about one another, speaking evil of other people. I am afraid I may find you full of pride and out of harmony among yourselves. [21] I am so afraid that when I come, God will make me feel ashamed of you. I am afraid I shall be full of sorrow about those who have kept on with their old sins. I am afraid I shall find that some have never stopped their low sex habits, the sins against good morals, the loose lives which they lived before they were Christians.

13 When I make this third visit I may have to pass judgment on some of these people. Any charge must be supported by the evidence of two or three witnesses. [2] While I was on my second visit I did not spare those who continued in sin. And I warn all who may be sinning while I am away that I will not spare them when I come again. [3] Do you need more proof than this that Christ is really speaking through me? When I come to Corinth, Christ will not be weak in dealing with you. You will see His power among you. [4] Christ was weak when He was put

to death on the cross. But now He lives again by the power of God. I am weak as Christ was weak, but in dealing with you I shall have the power of God because I live in Christ.

[5] So put yourselves on trial. Examine yourselves to see whether you are holding your faith. Do you not understand that Christ dwells in you? If not, you fail to pass the test. [6] I hope you will begin to see that we have not failed the test. [7] I pray God that you may not do wrong. I pray this not because I want people to call me a success in my work. No, not that. I pray that you may do right, no matter how much any one may tell you that I have failed. [8] No matter what any one says about me, I must work only for the truth, never against it. [9] If you are strong, I am glad even though I am weak. What I pray for is that you may grow better and better. [10] I write all this to you while I am away so that, when I come, I may not need to be severe. The Lord gave me this authority not to tear you down but to build you up.

[11] Now, brothers, good-bye. Make every wrong among you right, do what I ask you, agree with one another, live in peace. And the God of love and peace will be with you. [12] Greet one another for me with a holy kiss. [13] All God's people send you their best wishes.

[14] The grace of the Lord Jesus Christ, and the love of God and the warm friendship of the Holy Spirit remain with all of you.

Paul
Timothy

PAUL'S LETTER
TO THE CHRISTIANS IN GALATIA

From: *Paul, an apostle of Jesus Christ*

To: *The Churches of Galatia*

1   I was made an apostle by Jesus Christ and by God the Father who raised Christ from the dead. I was not chosen by any man to be an apostle, but only by God.

² All the brothers who are here join me in sending greetings to their fellow Christians in Galatia.

³ May God our Father and our Lord Jesus Christ give you grace and peace. ⁴ Christ gave His life for our sins. He died to save us from this evil world. This He did because it was the will of God our Father. ⁵ To Him be glory for ever and ever. Amen.

⁶ When I was with you, I said that Christ called you because of His great loving kindness. But I am shocked to hear that you are already deserting my Good News and turning to another message. ⁷ There is no other true Good News than that which I gave you. But I hear that other men are troubling you and are trying to change the message which I preached to you about Christ. ⁸ This is terrible. Why, if we or even an angel from heaven should preach a message contrary to that which I gave you, a curse will be on him. For God himself gave me this message, and it must never be changed. ⁹ So I repeat what you heard me say before: If any man preaches a message which opposes the Good News which you received from me, God's curse will be on him.

¹⁰ Does this sound as though I am trying to win the favor of men, or the favor of God? Am I trying to please men? Oh no! If I were trying to please men, I would never have become Christ's slave.

[11] I want you to know, brothers, that the Good News which I preached to you did not come from men. [12] I did not receive it from any other man. No one taught it to me. It was revealed to me by Jesus Christ.

[13] You have heard the story of my life before I became a Christian. I punished the church of God with mad hate and I tried to destroy it. [14] I was away ahead of most young men of my age in the Jewish religion. I was full of burning zeal for the rules and customs handed down from old times by our fathers. [15] But God had chosen me for His work even before I was born. One day in His great grace He called me. [16] He revealed His Son to me; then He sent me out to preach Christ to the Gentiles.

When Christ spoke to me, I did not ask advice from any one. [17] I did not go up to Jerusalem to see those who had become apostles before me. I went away into Arabia and then later I returned to Damascus. [18] It was not until three years later that I went up to Jerusalem to see Peter. I stayed with him fifteen days. [19] The only other apostle I saw on that visit was James the brother of the Lord. [20] Before God I will take oath that this is the exact truth. [21] I went from there into the district of Syria and Cilicia. [22] Nobody in the churches of Christ in Judea even knew what I looked like. [23] They had only heard it said, "The man who used to punish and kill us is now preaching the faith which he had tried to destroy." [24] They praised God for the way I had changed.

2 Fourteen years later I again went up to Jerusalem, this time with Barnabas. I took Titus the Greek along with me, too. [2] I went because Christ told me to go. In Jerusalem I explained to them the Good News which I preached to the Gentiles. I did this in a private meeting with the church leaders. I wanted to make sure that what I had preached and planned to preach would not be lost. [3] They approved of it, and though Titus was a Greek, yet they did not require him to be circumcised. [4] But

some false brothers came to the meeting in secret. Their plan was to destroy the liberty we have in Christ Jesus and to make us slaves again to the old law. [5] But I did not yield to them even for a moment. I kept the Good News true for you Gentiles. [6] Those who were supposed to be the church leaders did not add a thing to my Good News. What office they held in the church makes no difference to me. God takes no account of a man's office.

[7] God had chosen Peter to preach the Good News to the circumcised Jews. They began to realize that God had also chosen me to preach the Good News to those who were not circumcised. [8] God had done a great work through me for the Gentiles, just as God had worked through Peter among the circumcised. [9] When James and Peter and John, the church leaders, saw how God had given me His grace, they gave Barnabas and me the right hand of friendship as their brothers in the work. They told us to go to the Gentiles, while they would work with the circumcised. [10] The only thing they suggested was that we should remember the poor—and I was eager to do that very thing.

[11] Later Peter came up to visit Antioch. There I had to oppose him to his face because his actions were false. [12] At first he ate with the Gentiles. But when some of James' men came, Peter separated himself from the Gentiles. He was afraid of those Jewish Christians. [13] Then all the other Jewish Christians played false as Peter did, for they also kept away from the Gentiles. Even Barnabas was carried away by their false actions. [14] But when I saw that they were not honest and straight about the truth of the Good News, I said to Peter before them all: "What does this mean? Though you are a Jew yet you live like the Gentiles, not like the Jews. Why, then, do you try to make the Gentiles live like Jews? [15] You are Jews by birth as I am. We are not Gentiles. [16] Yet we know that not one of us is made just by obeying our Jewish law. We are saved through faith in Christ Jesus. We Jews have to believe Jesus Christ in order to be saved, just as the Gentiles do. We have been saved by

faith in Christ, not by obeying our law. Nobody is saved by the law." That is what I told Peter. [17] And it is true. We Jews were found guilty by the law just as much as the Gentiles were. There is no way for us to get right with God except through Christ.

Does this mean that Christ allows us to go on sinning then? Certainly not; Christ sets us free from sin.

[18] But I ask you: Shall I now go back and depend once more upon keeping the laws of Moses? No! For I am sure to break some of those laws, and then I shall be guilty. [19] The law of Moses said that I had to die. Through Christ I did die—I died to the law! To the law I am dead, but to God I am alive. [20] I mean this: Christ took me to the cross with him, and I died there with him. It is no longer I that live. Christ is living in me. It is true that I am still living in the flesh. But I live now by faith in the Son of God who loved me and gave His life to save me. [21] I will not be so foolish as to refuse the mercy which God offered me. Christ died to set me free from sin. But if I could have been made just by obeying the law, Christ would have died for nothing.

3   Oh, you foolish men of Galatia! Who has cast a wicked spell over you? Do you not remember when I taught you that Christ died on the cross to save you? [2] Do you not remember how the Holy Spirit came upon you? Now let me ask you: Did you receive the Holy Spirit because you were keeping the law of Moses? No! The Holy Spirit came because you heard and believed the Good News of Christ. [3] How can you be so foolish now? You began with the Holy Spirit. Are you ending up by going back to those laws which bring only death? [4] Haven't you learned anything from all you suffered? I cannot believe you will fail now. [5] God gave you His Holy Spirit and He works miracles among you. Does He work them because you obey the law of Moses? No, it is because you believe the message of Christ.

⁶ It was the same way with Abraham.

"He believed God and that is why God counted
him just."

⁷ Who are the real sons of Abraham? They are the men who have faith like Abraham had. ⁸ Our Holy Writings said long ago that God would count the Gentiles to be just if they had faith. Long, long ago God told Abraham:

"Through you all the Gentiles shall be blessed."

And it is true! ⁹ All men who have faith receive the same blessing that Abraham received.

¹⁰ But all those who depend on obeying the law are under a curse. For it is written:

"Every one is cursed if he does not obey all the things
written in the book of the law."

¹¹ No man ever was able to keep all the law. So the law never made any man just in God's sight.

Our holy books say:

"He whose faith makes him right with God shall live."

¹² Yet the law of Moses does not accept faith; it says you must obey all the law, or you die! It is written:

"Only he that does all that the law commands shall live."

So the law puts the curse of death on us all. ¹³ Christ has bought us from that curse. He bought us by being cursed for us on the cross. It is written

"Cursed be every one who hangs on a tree."

¹⁴ So Jesus Christ by dying on the tree gave you Gentiles the blessing which God promised Abraham that you should have. God kept His promise with you Gentiles. You know that when you put your faith in Christ, the Holy Spirit came upon you.

¹⁵ Perhaps I can make this clearer by an example from our daily life. After a man makes a will and signs it, nobody can add

to it or take away from it. [16] The agreement which God made with Abraham is like that. The agreement was made with Abraham and his "seed." It does not say "seeds," as if it meant many sons, but "seed," meaning one Son. This one Son is Christ.

[17] Now notice my point carefully. There was no law of Moses when God made this agreement with Abraham. That law came four hundred and thirty years later. The law did not add a thing to God's agreement with Abraham nor take a thing from it. [18] If we had been saved by Moses' law, the agreement with Abraham would have been ended. But the law does not save us. We are saved by the agreement God made with Abraham, and by that agreement alone.

[19] Why, then, did God give Moses the law? It was added because men sinned and needed to have their sin made plain to them. It lasted until the "seed," that is Christ, arrived—the Christ Whom God had promised.

I have noticed an interesting fact. The law was sent down to earth through different messengers. The angels and Moses brought it from God to man. [20] But the agreement of God with Abraham had no messengers in between. God gave it directly to Abraham.

[21] Is the law, then, opposed to the promise which God made to Abraham? Certainly not. If the law had been able to give life, then we would be right with God through keeping it. But no, the law cannot save us. It has another purpose. [22] The law was given to warn us. It warns us all that we deserve to die because we have sinned. That warning makes us seek the other way to be saved—the way of faith. It drives us to believe in Jesus Christ.

[23] Before faith in Christ came, the law was our guard. It kept us under its control until faith in Christ came. [24] The law was like a servant guarding us children until Christ came. Then He made us right with God, through our faith in Him. [25] Christ has brought us faith, so we no longer need a servant to guard us. [26] Because we put our faith in Christ Jesus we are all sons of God. [27] All of you who were baptized into Christ, are now

clothed in Christ. ²⁸ In Christ there must be no divisions. There
is no Jew or Greek, no slave or freeman, no man or woman;
you are all one in Christ Jesus. ²⁹ If you are Christ's, you are
the real children of Abraham, and so you are heirs of the promise
God made to him.

4   This is what I mean. When an heir is still a boy under age
he is like a servant. Although he is really the owner of the
property, ² yet he is under guards and managers until the date
set by his father. ³ We are like that. When we were children we
were treated as servants. We were learning the ABC's of this
world.

⁴ But at the right time God sent His Son who was born by
a woman. He was born under the law. ⁵ He paid the price to set
free from sin all of us who had been guarded by the law. He
came to clear the way for us to be adopted as sons of God. ⁶ Now
you are God's sons. God has sent the Spirit of His Son into your
hearts. There the Spirit keeps saying, "Father, dear Father."
⁷ You, my brother, are no longer a slave under a guard. You
are a son! And if you are a son, you are also an heir of God!

⁸ In former days when you did not know God, you were under
control of gods which really were not gods at all. ⁹ But you have
come to know God. And even better, God knows and accepts you.

Why, then, I ask, are you so ready to turn back to the old
poor vain rule of laws? Do you want to become slaves under
a guard again? ¹⁰ Why have you once more begun to keep those
special days and months and seasons and years named in the
law? ¹¹ I am afraid for you. Has my labor with you all been
wasted? ¹² I beg of you to remain free from the law, just as I
am. Though I am a Jew, yet I became free from the law, just
as you Gentiles always were.

I do not mean to say that you have ever wronged me. Oh no,
just the opposite! ¹³ You saw how sick I was when I first
preached the Good News to you. ¹⁴ My condition was a trial to
you, and yet you never laughed at me or slighted me. No, you

treated me like an angel of God, or like Christ Jesus Himself. [15] I can bear witness that if you could you would have torn out your eyes and given them to me. Where has all this joy gone which you had in me then? [16] Have I made you my enemy by telling you the truth?

[17] These other men who are courting your favor are doing it for no good purpose. They are trying to turn you against me so that you will court only them. [18] But I want you and me to court one another all the time, not only when I am there with you. I want this for your own good.

[19] Oh, my little children, I am suffering a mother's birth pains all over again until you take Christ back into your heart. I am in great suffering because of you. [20] How I wish I could be there with you now and change my tone. I am very much worried about you.

[21] Tell me, now, do you know what you are doing when you desire to go back under the law of Moses? You had better study that law. [22] Our Holy Book says that Abraham had two sons, one by a slave woman and one by a free woman. [23] The son of the slave woman was born in the usual natural way. But the son of the free woman was born because of God's promise. [24] These two women are representatives of the two kinds of agreements which God has made with men. One agreement came from Mt. Sinai and gives birth only to slaves. This is Hagar. [25] Hagar the slave woman stands for Mt. Sinai, down in Arabia where Moses got the law. Hagar also represents the present-day Jerusalem, for the Jews are still slaves to the law that came from Mt. Sinai. [26] But Sarah, who was Abraham's free woman, represents the Jerusalem in heaven, and she is the mother of all of us who believe in Christ.

[27] This is what God's Word means when it says to Sarah:

"Be glad, O woman who bears no child.
Break forth and shout, you who have had no birth
pains;

101

for you whose husband has left you alone
shall have more children than the one who has
your husband."

28 Now, my brothers, we are like Isaac. He was a child of
the promise, and we too are children of the promise. 29 The child
who was born the natural way ill-treated the child who was born
by the Spirit of God. This same thing is true today. The sons of
Hagar ill-treat us in the same way.

30 The holy writings say, "Put away the slave woman and her
son, for her son shall not be heir along with the son of the free
woman." 31 My brothers, we who follow Christ are not slave
children. We are the children of the free woman.

5 Christ has set us free. He means us to stay free. So stay free
and do not let anybody make a slave of you again. 2 Listen to
me while I, Paul, warn you. Do not let them circumcise you. If
you let them circumcise you, Christ can no longer help you. 3 I
warn you that any man who lets them circumcise him, has got
to obey all the rest of the law from Mt. Sinai, or he will die.
4 If you depend on the law to save you, you cut yourself off
from Christ and from the mercy of God which alone can save you.

5 When you and I believed, we received God's Spirit. And this
makes us sure that we will be right with God. 6 When you are
in Christ Jesus, God does not ask whether you are circumcised
or not. He asks you only to have faith and love.

7 You were doing so well! Who influenced you to leave the
truth? 8 Certainly God did not. 9 Remember the saying: "A little
yeast will make the whole dough rise." 10 I believe with all my
heart that you will give up that wrong teaching. I believe you
will come back to mine. And I warn you, the man who was
troubling you, whoever he is, will receive God's judgment. 11 Do
I tell people to be circumcised? Never! Is that not the very reason
they are ill-treating me? If I taught people to be circumcised,
the Jews would no longer object to the cross. 12 I wish those who

cause you so much worry about being circumcised would finish the job and cut off all their own private parts.

[13] Brothers, you were called to be free. But be careful not to use your freedom to satisfy the passions of your flesh. Use your freedom to serve one another in love. [14] All the law is summed up in one sentence: "Love your neighbor as yourself." [15] You who bite or try to eat one another are not free. You who act that way had better take care or you will destroy one another.

[16] But I say, walk in the Spirit and do not try to satisfy the passions of the flesh. [17] For the flesh has desires which are against the Spirit. And the Spirit has desires which are against the flesh. They are opposed to one another. So you cannot do everything you feel like doing. [18] But if you are guided by the Spirit you live above the law.

[19] The things which our lower nature tempts us to do are plain: They are sins of sex, evil passions, loose living, [20] worshiping idols, magic, hate, quarreling, being jealous or angry or selfish, having party divisions and party fights, [21] envy, having rough drinking parties and getting drunk—things like these. I warned you and I warn you again: Those who do such things will not have any place in the Kingdom of God. [22] But when the Spirit bears its fruit we have love, joy, and peace of heart. [23] We are patient, kind, good, faithful, gentle, and we practice self-control. There is no law against these things. [24] Those who belong to Christ Jesus have nailed the flesh on the cross with its passions and desires. [25] If we live in the Spirit let us be guided by the Spirit.

[26] Do not be vain, do not make one another angry, and do not envy one another.

6 Brothers, if a man is tempted and does wrong, you who have the Spirit of Christ should help him get right again in a gentle spirit. Watch yourself, for you may be tempted, too. [2] Bear one another's burdens, for that is the way to carry out Christ's law of love.

[3] If anybody thinks he is important when he is nobody, he is fooling himself. [4] Each one of us ought to test his own work. Then he will have reason to take joy in his own work, and not just in talking about his neighbor's work. [5] Every man must carry his share of the load.

[6] And you who are being taught the Good News must help support those who teach you.

[7] Do not deceive yourselves; you cannot fool God. Whatever a man sows he will gather at the harvest time. [8] He who sows to satisfy his flesh will gather only death and decay. He who sows the Spirit will receive everlasting life. [9] So let us not grow tired of doing good. When the time comes, if we do not lose heart, we shall gather a good harvest. [10] So let us do good to all men whenever we have a chance. Let us do good especially to those who belong to the family of our Christian faith.

[11] I, Paul, am ending this letter with my own hand-writing. See what large letters I am making.

[12] Do you know why those men are trying to force you to be circumcised? It is because they want to make a good showing to the world. They want to save themselves from suffering for the cross of Christ. [13] Those who are circumcised do not keep all the law. But they want you to be circumcised so that they can boast that they had you do it. [14] As for me, I shall never boast about anything except the cross of our Lord Jesus Christ. On his cross the world died to me and I died to the world. [15] Being circumcised means nothing and not being circumcised means nothing. It is the new birth that means everything.

[16] Peace and mercy be upon all of you who are guided by this higher law. You are the true children of Abraham, the true Israel of God.

[17] From now on let no man trouble me. I carry wounds on my body that prove that I am a slave of Jesus.

[18] The grace of our Lord Jesus Christ be with your spirit, my brothers. Amen.

Paul

PAUL'S LETTER
TO THE CHRISTIANS IN EPHESUS
(From Prison in Rome)

From: *Paul, apostle of Christ Jesus, by God's will*

To: *God's people in Ephesus*

1 I am writing to all the Christians of Ephesus who have remained faithful to Christ Jesus.

² May our Father God and our Lord Jesus Christ give you grace and peace.

³ I praise God the Father of our Lord Jesus Christ because He sent Christ to bless us. And Christ has blessed us with heaven's every blessing.

⁴ Even before God laid the foundation of the world He had chosen us. He had planned that we were to be holy and free from blame in His sight. ⁵ He had planned that we should be His sons through Jesus Christ. That was His loving will; that was His plan. ⁶ That was why He sent to us the Son whom He loved. Praise God for His wonderful grace. ⁷ The blood of Christ paid for us and now we belong to Him. We had broken God's law, but He forgave us. ⁸ So rich in mercy was God's love toward us!

⁹ And now God has let us know His secret plan. It is built around Christ. ¹⁰ The plan is this: God plans, when the right time comes, to unite everything in heaven and on earth in Christ. ¹¹ Whatever God plans to do He always does. ¹² He had already chosen us long before we put our hope in Christ. He had planned that we should live and praise Him for His glory.

¹³ You also in Ephesus heard this glorious truth, this Good News that Jesus could save you. You believed in Christ. He gave you the Holy Spirit which He had promised. That is how God sealed His choice of you. ¹⁴ The Holy Spirit is the first proof that some day we are to be God's heirs. At last God will give

us all that He has promised us, and we shall praise Him for His glory.

[15] I have heard of your faith in the Lord Jesus and your love for all of God's people. [16] I never stop thanking God for you. I keep praying for you [17] to the God of our Lord Jesus Christ, the Father of Glory. I pray that He may give you wisdom and more knowledge about Him. [18] I pray that your eyes may be open to see how wonderful is the hope to which God called you. I pray that you may see what rich glory God plans to give to all His people. [19] I pray that you may realize that His power in us who believe, is great beyond all measure. It is the same mighty power [20] that worked in Christ. By that power God raised Him from the dead and had Him sit at His right hand in heaven. [21] There Jesus sits above all rulers, above all authority, above all power, above all lords. He is above every name both in this age and in the age to come. [22] God has put all things under Christ's feet. God has made Christ the head of everything in the church. [23] The church is His body and it is filled with Him. Indeed, everything God has created is filled with Christ.

2 You were dead because you sinned and broke God's law. But now Christ has made you alive. [2] You once followed the ways of the world. The world follows the prince of evil spirits who is working in those who break God's laws. [3] We all once lived among those who lead an evil life. Like them we obeyed the passions of the flesh. We yielded to the evil desires of our bodies and to our evil thoughts. Because of this we deserved God's punishment like everybody else. [4] But God is rich in mercy and He felt a great love for us. [5] We were dead because of our sins but God brought us back to life again with Christ. By His mercy we have been saved. [6] He raised us from the dead with Christ so that we shall sit with Christ in heaven in the coming ages. [7] Through Christ, God will pour out His kindness upon us. He will show us how rich beyond words is His grace to us.

[8] You who have put your faith in Him were saved by His

grace. You did nothing to deserve it. It was God's gift. ⁹ You did not earn it by your good work; so no one can boast about that. ¹⁰ He made us all over new. We were born again in Christ. Now our work is to do the good deeds which God has intended us to do.

¹¹ Remember that you were Gentiles by birth. The Jews who were circumcised by human hands say that you were not circumcised. ¹² As long as you were separated from Christ, you were shut out from the Jews, God's chosen people. You had no share in those agreements and promises which God made with the Jews. You had no hope and no God in the world. ¹³ You were far from God. But you have been brought into God's family by the blood of Christ.

¹⁴ He is our peace. He has brought the Jews and the Gentiles together. He broke down the wall between the Jews and Gentiles. ¹⁵ By giving His life He put an end to the Jewish law with its commands and rules. He made peace between Jews and Gentiles by creating one new man instead of two. ¹⁶ Christ made Jews and Gentiles into one body by giving His one body for us on the cross. He made us both friends of God. Thus He ended the hate between us. ¹⁷ He came with this Good News of peace between you Gentiles who were far from God and us Jews who were near God. ¹⁸ Through Christ you Gentiles and we Jews have one Spirit and can come to the Father together. ¹⁹ You Gentiles are no longer strangers in a foreign land. You are now citizens of His Kingdom. You are the people of God. You are members of God's family.

²⁰ You are like a building which has the apostles and prophets as its foundation. Jesus Christ Himself is the chief cornerstone. ²¹ Christ is joining us all together to build a holy temple of the Lord. ²² You are all being built into this temple where the Spirit of God Himself lives.

3 This is why I, Paul, am a prisoner. Christ Jesus has made me a prisoner for the sake of you Gentiles. ² No doubt you have

heard how God in His loving kindness made me a minister to you. [3] I have written a little about this to you already. I told you how God had revealed His secret to me. [4] As you read what I am writing, you will see how I came to know the mystery of Christ. [5] This mystery had not been told to people in past centuries. But now the Spirit of God has revealed it to His holy apostles and prophets. [6] It is the Good News that through Jesus Christ, the Gentiles are now fellow heirs with the Jews. We are now all members of the same body. Now we all share the same promise.

[7] God made me a minister of this Good News. God gave me His grace and He has worked with power in me. [8] Though I am the very least of all God's people, yet God did me this great favor. He chose me to preach to the Gentiles the wealth of Christ which is far greater than we can ever know. [9] God chose me to help men everywhere to see His secret plan. This plan has been hidden for ages in the mind of God who created all things. [10] But now through us in His church, He is revealing His deep wisdom even to the princes and powers of heaven. [11] God had this plan before the world began, and now He has carried it out through Jesus Christ our Lord. [12] Now we who have faith in Christ dare to go to God with perfect confidence. [13] So, brothers, I beg of you not to lose heart on account of my sufferings. I am suffering for you. Glory in it.

[14] When I think of the Father's great plan, I bow my knees before Him. [15] By Him every family in heaven and on earth was given its name. [16] I pray that out of the wealth of His glory He may pour His spirit into you and make you strong. [17] I pray that through your faith Christ may dwell in your hearts. I pray that the roots of your faith may grow deep in the ground of His love. [18] I pray that you and all God's people may see how wide and long and high and deep His love is. [19] I pray that you may know this love of Christ which goes beyond our understanding. I pray that you may be completely filled with God.

[20] When God's power is working in us, He can do far more than we dare ask or even think. [21] May the church give God glory for Christ Jesus through all the ages to come. Amen.

4 I, a prisoner for the Lord's sake, beg you to lead a life worthy of your high calling. [2] Be humble and gentle. Be patient and make allowances for one another, because you love one another. [3] Be eager to remain one in the Spirit. Be at peace with one another. [4] We who are in Christ ought to be one; we are one body; there is only one Holy Spirit; you are all called to only one hope. It is the same hope for you all. [5] You have only one Lord and one faith and one baptism. [6] You have only one God who is the Father of us all. He is above us all. He is in us all. He works through us all.

[7] God shows His loving kindness to each one of us. It is so great that we can measure it only by the gift of Christ. [8] That is why God's Word says:

"When He went up on high
He led great numbers out of prison
and He gave His gifts to men."

[9] You notice that it says "He went up on high." It must also mean that He went down to the lower parts of the world. [10] He went down to the lowest and up to the highest so that He could fill everything and everybody everywhere with Himself.

[11] He gives us different kinds of gifts. He made some of us apostles, some of us preachers, some of us missionaries, some of us ministers and teachers. [12] Each of these was chosen to train God's people to serve and so to build up the body of Christ. [13] Through them God works to unite us all in faith and knowledge of the Son of God. He works until all of us are grown up in spirit to the full height of Christ.

[14] Then we shall no longer be like children. We shall not be blown back and forth and turned round and round by every new wind of teaching. We shall no longer be deceived by men who

come with smart tricks and lies. [15] No, we shall all tell the truth in a loving spirit.

And we shall all grow up as a part of Christ, who is our head. [16] The whole body of the church is joined to Him and each part is joined to every other. Each part of the church is working better and better, as the whole church grows and builds itself up in love.

[17] So I tell you this, and I say it from the Lord. You must no longer live like the Gentiles with their futile thoughts. [18] Their minds are in darkness. They are strangers separated from God's life by their ignorance and their hard hearts. [19] Their consciences are dull. They have given themselves over to sex vices. They burn to practice dirty habits. [20] You did not learn anything like that from Christ. [21] You are in Jesus. You have been taught the truth about Him. [22] You must throw away the old nature with its bad habits. It was like old clothes dirtied by evil passions. [23] You must be made all new in your mind and spirit. [24] And you must put on the fresh dress of your new nature which is fashioned right and holy like God Himself. [25] Throw away all lies. Tell the truth, every one to his neighbor, for we are members of one another. [26] If you get angry, do not sin. Get over your anger quickly. Never let the sun set on your anger. [27] For you must not give the devil a chance.

[28] If any one of you has been a thief, stop stealing. Go to work and make an honest living with your hands. Then you will be able to help anybody who is in need.

[29] Let no evil talk come out of your mouth. Say only things which are good for building people up. Say whatever is fitting for each occasion. Say what will bless those who hear you. [30] Do nothing to pain the Holy Spirit of God. For the Holy Spirit in you is the proof and the seal that you are saved. [31] Throw away bitter words and quarrels and anger. Avoid loud talk or any talk at all that hurts other people. Throw away all ill will.

[32] Be kind and tender-hearted. Forgive one another just as God through Christ forgave you.

5 Follow God's example as His dear children. ² Be loving toward others as Christ was loving toward us. He gave His life for us, like a sweet-smelling sacrifice offered to God to save us.

³ Such things as sex sins and evil passions or envy of what others possess, should never even be named among you. The people of God should not talk about such things. ⁴ Dirty stories and bad jokes are not fit for you to use. Instead of using such language, give thanks to God!

⁵ Be sure of this: No man whose morals are bad or whose thoughts are not clean will be an heir of the Kingdom of Christ and God. People who worship idols do such things. ⁶ Do not let anybody's false arguments fool you about this. Vices like these bring down God's anger upon those who refuse to obey Him. ⁷ So have nothing to do with those people. ⁸ Once it was all dark within you, but now the Lord is in you and you are full of light. Live as children of the light. ⁹ Light always produces fruits which are good and right and true.

¹⁰ Find out what the Lord wants you to do. ¹¹ Take no part in what men do in the darkness. Their deeds bear no real fruit. Instead of doing those evil things, you must bring them out into the light. ¹² I am ashamed even to speak of the things which bad men do in secret. ¹³ But if anything bad is lifted out into the light it will be seen. Where it is seen it goes away like darkness and the light takes its place. ¹⁴ That is why we hear it said:

> Awake, you who are asleep.
> Arise from the dead,
> and Christ will give you light.

¹⁵ Take care then how you live. Do not be a fool; be wise. ¹⁶ These are evil days, and you must make the best use you can of your time. ¹⁷ Do not do foolish things, but understand what the Lord's will is. ¹⁸ Do not get drunk with wine, for that is wrong. Be filled with the Spirit. ¹⁹ Tell each other your joys with psalms and hymns and spirit-filled songs. Sing and make sweet

music to the Lord with all your hearts. [20] Always thank God the Father for everything in the name of our Lord Jesus Christ.

[21] Serve one another and so honor Christ. [22] Wives, obey your husbands as you would obey the Lord. [23] For the husband is the head of the wife just as Christ is the head of the church. The church is Christ's body, and He is the one Who saves it. [24] As the church is subject to Christ, so let wives be subject in everything to their husbands.

[25] Husbands, love your wives in the way Christ loves the church. He gave Himself up to die for her. [26] That is how He made the church holy. He made her clean by washing her with water and by teaching her. [27] He wants the church to be presented before Him in all her beauty, with no spots or wrinkles. He wants her to be holy and without a fault. [28] So husbands ought also to love their wives as they love their own bodies. The man who loves his wife is really loving himself. [29] No one hates his own flesh. He feeds it and takes care of it. Christ also feeds and takes care of His body, which is the church. [30] We are parts of Christ's body. [31] Our holy writings say:

"For this reason a man shall leave his father and his
    mother and be joined to his wife.
The two shall become one flesh."

[32] There is a secret truth in that saying. It means a man and his wife, but it also means the marriage of Christ to His church.

[33] So I say that each one of you must love his wife as himself; and the wife must respect her husband.

6 Children, you must obey your parents. This is right; it is what the Lord commanded. [2] The first command of God that had a promise with it, was this: "Honor your father and your mother. [3] Then it will be well for you in life and you will live long on the earth."

[4] Fathers, do not make your children angry. Bring them up well by teaching them and training them to follow the Lord.

⁵ Slaves, you must obey your human masters. Honor and respect them with all your heart. Do it as though you were serving Christ. ⁶ Work well, even when men's eyes are not on you. Work not only to please men. You are slaves of Christ, so do God's will from your hearts. ⁷ Do all your work with good will. Do it as you would for the Lord, not just for men. ⁸ You can be sure that whatever good a man does, God pays him back, whether he is a slave or free.

⁹ Masters, you must treat your slaves in the same spirit. Do not threaten them. Remember that the Lord in heaven is their Lord and yours. God shows no respect for a man's social position.

¹⁰ Finally, be strong in the Lord's strength, not your own. Get your power from Him. ¹¹ Put on all the armor of God. Then you will be able to stand up strong against the clever attacks of the devil.

¹² Our struggle is not against flesh and blood. It is against the rulers of the present dark world and it is against evil powers in the spirit world. ¹³ So put on all the armor of God. Then you will be able to stand firm when days are evil, and to hold your ground to the end. ¹⁴ Therefore stand firm. Wear truth like a belt around your body. And protect your breast with right living. ¹⁵ Put on the Good News of peace as shoes on your feet. ¹⁶ Above all, take faith for your shield. With faith you can stop all the burning arrows of the evil one. ¹⁷ To protect your head, put on the helmet of God's saving power. For your sword, take God's Spirit, which is His Word. ¹⁸ Pray at all times as the Spirit guides you. Keep wide awake and never give up. Keep praying in everything you do and ask God to help others. Never stop praying for all of God's people. ¹⁹ Pray for me, too, that when I open my mouth, the right words may be given to me. Pray that I may have courage to tell the secret truths of our Good News. ²⁰ Pray that I may declare the truth without fear, as I should. I am in chains because I dared to be a minister of Christ.

²¹ Tychicus is carrying this letter to you. He will tell you how

I am and what I am doing. He is my dear brother and a faithful minister for the Lord. He will tell you about everything. [22] I am sending him to you so that you may know how we all are, and so that he may encourage your hearts.

[23] Peace and love with faith be to all our brothers from God the Father and the Lord Jesus Christ. [24] God's grace be upon all of you who have a never-dying love for our Lord Jesus Christ.

Paul

PAUL'S LETTER
TO THE CHRISTIANS IN PHILIPPI
(From Prison in Rome)

From: *Paul*

To: *The Christians in Philippi:*

1 Timothy joins me in writing this letter to you. We are servants of Christ Jesus. We write to the bishops and deacons and all God's people in Philippi who belong to Jesus Christ.

[2] Grace and peace be to you from God our Father and from our Lord Jesus Christ.

[3] I thank God whenever I think of you. [4] My prayers for you are always full of joy. [5] I thank God for the way you worked with me in spreading the Good News from the first day I was with you until now. [6] I am sure that He who began such good work in you, will complete it on the day when Jesus Christ comes. [7] I have every reason to feel very happy about you. I hold you all in my heart. I never forget how you are sharing God's grace with me. You are sharing it with me while I am here in prison. While I was defending the Good News and proving it is true, I remembered how you shared it with me.

[8] God is my witness how I long to be with you again. I love you just as Jesus Christ loves you. [9] And I pray that your love

may keep on growing ever greater. I pray that your knowledge and understanding may keep growing. ¹⁰ I pray that you may always support every good thing. I pray that you may be pure in heart and without blame, on the day when Christ comes. ¹¹ I pray that you may be like a tree filled with the fruits of right living and right thinking. Jesus Christ will help you grow these fruits for God's glory and praise.

¹² I want you to know, brothers, that my being here in prison has helped the Good News spread. ¹³ All the soldiers who guard me and all the rest of the people in the Emperor's palace know that I am in prison because I preach Christ. ¹⁴ Because I am in prison, most of the Christian brothers have had their faith in Christ made stronger. They have more courage. They speak the word of God without fear.

¹⁵ Some, it is true, are preaching Christ with a spirit of envy and are opposing me. ¹⁶ But the others who have good will, are preaching in love. They know that I am in prison because I defend the Good News. ¹⁷ Those who oppose me are not sincere when they preach Christ. They are dividing the church into parties. Perhaps they wish to add to my sufferings here in prison.

¹⁸ But what does that matter? Christ is being preached whether they are sincere or not. That fills me with joy. ¹⁹ Yes, and I am going right on being full of joy. I have your prayers, and the Spirit of Jesus Christ is here helping me. And I know that in the end I shall be saved.

²⁰ My eager hope is that I shall never be ashamed. I want to have the courage to honor Christ to the end as I am doing now, whether I live or am put to death. ²¹ For me to live is Christ, and to die is gain. ²² If I live any longer in this body it will be only so that I can do useful work for Christ. I cannot tell which to choose, life or death. ²³ I am pulled in two directions. I want to go and be with Christ. That will be far better. ²⁴ But I think He needs me more here in this body for your sakes. ²⁵ I am sure you need me. So I expect to remain and continue to help you

to grow and to be happy in your faith. ²⁶ I hope that you will have every cause to praise Christ Jesus when I come to you again.

²⁷ So now, be sure to lead a life worthy of the Good News of Christ. Whether I come to see you or must be separated from you I want always to hear that you are standing firm. I want you to be united in spirit. I want you to stand side by side as you defend the faith in our Good News. ²⁸ Never be afraid of those who oppose you, no matter what they do. Your courage will be a clear sign to them that their way leads to ruin and that God will save you. ²⁹ You have been granted not only to believe in Christ, but also to suffer for His sake. ³⁰ You are in the same battle which you saw me fighting, and which I am still fighting, as you know.

2   Christ gives you courage. His love inspires you. You share in His Spirit. You feel His loving kindness and His sympathy.

² I know you want me to be perfectly happy about you. Then live in harmony with one another. Think as though you were one mind. Be united in love. ³ Do not be selfish nor proud. Be humble. Let each person think that others are better than himself. ⁴ Work for the interests of other people and not only for your own. ⁵ Treat other people in the way you learned from Christ. ⁶ Remember what Christ Himself did. He had the same nature as God. Yet He did not hold on to His high place with God. ⁷ He laid aside His true nature and became like a slave. He was born as a man. ⁸ Having become a man, He humbled himself. He obeyed God, all the way to death; yes, even to death on a cross. ⁹ That is why God has raised Him up on high. God has given Him the name above every name. ¹⁰ At the name of Jesus every knee shall bend, in Heaven and on earth and under the earth. ¹¹ Every tongue shall confess that Jesus Christ is Lord. And all shall praise God the Father.

¹² My dear ones, you have always obeyed God. You obeyed while I was with you. Now while I am away from you, show

by what you do, that you are truly saved. Always be careful for fear you may not please Him. [13] God is working in you to help you to do His will and to please Him.

[14] Do everything without complaining or arguing. [15] Be innocent and pure in heart. Be children of God without a fault, though you are in the midst of wicked, twisted people. You must shine among them like lights in a dark world. [16] Hold fast to the word of life. Then when Christ comes I shall feel proud that I did not run for nothing, and that I did not work for you in vain.

[17] Perhaps my lifeblood may soon be poured out as a sacrifice to God for your faith. If so, I am glad to go, and I shall thank God with you. [18] I want you to be glad, too, and to thank God.

[19] I hope by the help of the Lord Jesus to send Timothy to you soon. I want to be cheered by news from you. [20] I have no one else here like him, no one else who will take such real interest in your good. [21] The others are more interested in their own affairs than in the work of Jesus Christ. [22] But you all know how much Timothy is worth to me. Like a son for his father, he has worked with me for the Good News. [23] As soon as I learn how my case in court turns out, I will send Timothy to you. [24] And I trust in the Lord that before long I may come to you too.

[25] You sent Epaphroditus to me, and he has taken good care of me. He has been a brother to me, a fellow worker, and a fellow soldier. But I feel that I ought to send him back to you now. [26] He is anxious to see you all. He is troubled because you heard that he was sick. [27] Yes, he was very sick, so sick that he nearly died. But God had mercy on him. God had mercy on me too, for He did not add another sorrow to my sufferings. [28] I am eager to send Epaphroditus back to you because I know how glad you will be to see him home again. Knowing that he is home with you will make my sorrows lighter. [29] Give him a warm welcome in the Lord. Honor men like him. [30] He nearly died for the sake of Christ's work. He risked his life serving me as you yourselves were not able to do.

3 Now, my brothers, be full of joy in the Lord. I do not mind writing that advice over and over, and it is good for you to read it.

[2] I warn you, watch out for the dogs! Watch out for the men who are working evil. Watch out for the men who want to cut your flesh. [3] You and I are already truly circumcised in spirit. We have the Holy Spirit. We worship God and we glory in Christ Jesus. We do not put any confidence in circumcising the flesh.

[4] If any man thinks he has reasons to put his confidence in flesh, I have more reasons. [5] Look at my record. I was born a Jew. I was circumcised when I was eight days old. I belong to the tribe of Benjamin. I am a Hebrew and the son of Hebrews. I was a Pharisee and I obeyed the law as a Pharisee. [6] No one could find fault with the way I kept the law. I was so full of zeal that I tried to destroy the Church.

[7] But if I gained anything by this, I have counted it all as loss for the sake of Christ. [8] Indeed, I count everything in the world as loss for the greatest gain of all—the gain of knowing Christ Jesus my Lord. For His sake I have lost everything and count it as waste to be thrown away so that I may gain Christ [9] and be with Him.

I could never have got right with God by keeping the law. I put my faith in Christ, and He has made me right with God. The only right I have depends upon my faith in Christ. [10] I want to know Him and the power which raised Him from the dead. I am willing to share His sufferings and to die as He died, [11] so that I may rise again from the dead.

[12] I have not yet reached the highest life, nor am I yet perfect. But I keep pressing forward to make that life my own, just as Christ Jesus made me His own. [13] Brothers, I do not claim that I have hold of that highest life as yet. But one thing I do. Forgetting the things I have left behind, I reach forward to the things that are ahead. [14] I press on and up toward the finishing line. I am trying for the prize; God through Christ Jesus is calling me to come on up.

[15] Let all of us who are grown-up Christians keep our minds on this high purpose. Then if any of you have plans which interfere with God's highest purpose, He will reveal this to you. [16] But always hold true to what you do see. [17] Brothers, follow my example. And be guided only by those men who are following our example.

[18] I say this because so many people are enemies of the cross of Christ. I have often told you about them. I warn you now again with tears. [19] They will end in ruin. They worship their stomachs. They boast about things they ought to be ashamed of. They never think of anything above this world.

[20] But your country and mine is in Heaven. We are waiting for the Savior to come from Heaven. The Lord Jesus Christ when He comes, [21] will make our poor bodies all over again. He will make them like His glorious body. He will change us by His mighty power which brings the whole world under His rule.

4 My brothers, I love you; I long to be with you. You are my joy and my crown. Stand firm in the Lord, my dear ones.

[2] I beg Euodia and Syntyche to become good friends again in the Lord. [3] And I ask you, my true fellow worker, to help those two women. They worked side by side with me for the Good News. We all worked together with Clement and the rest of my fellow workers. Their names are all in the book of life.

[4] Be glad all the time in the Lord. I say again, be glad. [5] Let all men see how gentle and patient you are. The Lord is near. [6] Do not worry about anything. When you pray tell God about everything you want and give Him thanks. [7] Then God's peace, which passes all understanding, will guard your hearts and minds in Christ Jesus.

[8] Brothers, here is my last word. Whatever is true, whatever you hold in honor, whatever is right, whatever is pure, whatever is lovely, whatever has a good name, if anything is noble, if anything deserves praise, these are the things to think about. [9] Do as I taught you. Do what you learned, both by what you

heard from me and by what you saw me do. Then God's peace will be with you.

[10] For the gift you sent me I thank God with all my heart. It is a new proof of your deep concern for me. I always knew that you were concerned for me, but you had no way to show it. [11] I am not complaining that I have been in great want. In whatever condition I am I have learned to be content. [12] I know how to be poor and how to have plenty. I know how to be full and how to go hungry. I know how to have more than enough and how to have nothing. [13] I can do anything through Christ Who gives me strength.

[14] Yet you have been very kind to share my troubles once more. [15] You remember that in the early days in Philippi when I left Macedonia preaching the Good News, you were the only church that sent me any money. [16] Yes, more than once while I was in Thessalonica, you sent me help. [17] I am not looking for gifts, but I delight in the reward God will give you because you sent them to me. [18] I have received from Epaphroditus the gift you sent. It was like a sweet-smelling offering. It was the kind of sacrifice that God likes and accepts. I have enough and more than enough. I am filled!

[19] My God will supply every need of yours, for He has great riches in glory in Christ Jesus. [20] To God, our Father, be glory for ever and ever. Amen. [21] Greetings to every one of God's people who belong to Christ Jesus. [22] The brothers who are with me send you their greetings. All God's people here send greetings, and those who belong to Caesar's house send special greetings.

[23] May the grace of the Lord Jesus Christ be with your spirit.

Paul
Timothy

PAUL'S LETTER
TO THE CHRISTIANS IN COLOSSAE

(From Prison in Rome)

From: *Paul, whom God appointed as an apostle of Christ Jesus*

To: *The Christians in Colossae*

1 My brother Timothy joins me in writing this letter. ² We are writing to the people of God, our faithful brothers in Colossae. May God our Father give you His grace and peace.

³ We are praying for you to God the Father of our Lord Jesus Christ; and we always thank Him for you. ⁴ We have heard of your faith in Christ Jesus. We have heard how you love all the people of God. ⁵ We have heard how you hope for the reward which God has laid up for you in heaven. You learned about this when the truth of the Good News first came to you. ⁶ This Good News is spreading over all the world, and it is bearing fruit and growing. And it has been bearing fruit among you, too, since the first day you heard and understood it. It is the truth about God's grace. ⁷ You learned it from Epaphras, my dear fellow servant. He is my faithful minister of Christ to you. ⁸ Epaphras has told me about the love which the Holy Spirit put in your hearts.

⁹ From the day he told me about you, I have never stopped praying for you. I keep asking God that you may know His will for you fully. I am asking that He may fill you with wisdom and understanding of the Spirit. ¹⁰ I pray that you may lead a life worthy of the Lord. I pray that you may please Him in every way. I pray that all your good work may bear fruit. I pray that you may know God better and better. ¹¹ I pray to God in His glorious might to give you strength. I pray that you may be able to endure every trial with patience and joy. ¹² Thank God that He has made you ready, with all God's other people, to be heirs of His Kingdom of light. ¹³ He has freed us from the power

121

of darkness and has led us into the kingdom of His dear Son. [14] His Son has paid the price to set us free. Our sins are forgiven.

[15] Christ is exactly like God, whom we cannot see. Christ was born before anything was created. [16] It was through Christ that God created everything in heaven and on earth. Through Christ He created everything that we can see and everything that we cannot see. All the kingdoms, all the powers, all the princes and all the rulers, yes, everything was created through Christ and for Christ. [17] He was before all things. By Him all things are held together. [18] He is the head of the church, and the church is His body. He is the beginning of everything. He was the first to rise from the dead. So in everything He stands first. [19] In Christ the full nature of God was pleased to live. [20] God is working through Christ to make everything on earth and in heaven His friend again. When Christ poured out His blood on the cross He made peace between God and men.

[21] Once you too were strangers to God. Your thoughts were at war with God. Your deeds were evil. [22] But when Christ's body of flesh died on the cross, He made you friends of God once more. And Christ will present you holy and without fault or blame before God, [23] if you continue to have faith. But you must remain firm and steady. Let no one ever lead you away from the hope which you heard in the Good News. This Good News is being preached to every person under Heaven.

I, Paul, am a minister of this Good News. [24] And I am happy to suffer for your sakes. In my flesh I am completing Christ's sufferings for His church. The church is His body. [25] It was God who appointed me to be His minister to you. He sent me to preach His message everywhere. [26] He sent me to tell the secret plan which has been hidden for centuries and even for ages. Now at last that plan has been made plain to the people of God. [27] God chose me to tell you Gentiles what a rich, glorious secret this is for you. The secret is this:

"Christ in you is your hope of glory."

[28] He is the Christ I am preaching. I warn every one to accept Him, and I teach every one the wisdom God gave me. I want to help every man to become full grown in Christ. [29] This is what I am working for. I struggle with all the strength which He pours into me.

2 I want you to know how hard I am working and struggling for you. And I am working hard for the Christians in Laodicea and for all the other Christians who have never seen my face. [2] I pray that all your hearts may be full of courage. I pray that all of you may be bound together in love. I pray that all of you may be rich in your understanding of Christ. I pray that you may all fully know God's secret. [3] Christ is God's secret. All the treasures of wisdom and knowledge are hid in Him. [4] I am saying this because I hear that some people are trying to lead you the wrong way with fine sounding arguments.

[5] I am away from you in body, but I am with you in spirit. And I am very glad to hear that your churches are in good order and that your faith is firm in Christ. [6] Keep on living close to Christ Jesus the Lord as you did when you first received Him. [7] Be rooted in Him like a tree. Be built on Him like a house. Be strong in the faith which you were taught. [8] Do not let any one shake your faith. Some people are talking what they call "philosophy." They are telling lies. They tell stories which men made up about the spirits of this world. They do not follow Christ. [9] But in Christ and in Christ alone the whole of God dwells. [10] He only has all power and all authority. It is through Christ that your life has been filled full.

[11] And in Christ you have already been circumcised, but not with human hands. But when Christ circumcised you He cut away all your sinning body of flesh. [12] Yes, and when you were baptized you were buried with Christ. You believed in God's power to raise Jesus from the dead. And with Him you rose again from the dead. [13] Before you belonged to Christ you had been dead in your sins. Your flesh had never been circumcised.

But God forgave your sins and brought you back to life with Christ.

[14] God crossed out the whole debt against us in His account books. He no longer counted the laws that we had broken. He nailed the account book to the cross and closed the account.

[15] And He tore the swords from the hands of all the spirit rulers and the powers in the spirit world. He defeated them with Christ's cross. He showed how false they were.

[16] I do not want you to let any one worry you about what you shall eat or drink, or about keeping feasts, or new moons, or the old sabbath days. [17] Those customs are only the shadow of the real life which is coming. The real life comes from Christ. [18] So do not let any man lay down such rules for you. Do not let any one persuade you to humble yourselves before angels or worship them. It is foolish. Do not believe that man among you who is talking to you about his "visions." He is vain and without reason. He is only boasting about what he imagines. [19] He is not holding to Christ. Christ is our only Head. And from the Head the whole body of Christ is supplied with food. That body is the Church. It is joined together with joints and muscles, and God makes it grow.

[20] You died with Christ to this world. I ask you then why should you want to live as though you belonged to this world? Why should you put yourselves under the world's foolish rules? [21] They tell you: "Do not handle this. Do not taste that. Do not touch the other thing." [22] But these things are not holy. They all wear out after they are used a little while. Such rules and beliefs as these are not from God. They are made by men. [23] They may sound wise. They may make people seem religious. They may make people act as though they humbled themselves and put themselves under severe self-control. But they do not help at all to check the sins of the flesh.

3 You have been raised from the dead with Christ. So seek the things that are above, where Christ sits at the right hand of

God. [2] Love the things that are above, not the things of this earth. [3] For you died, and your life now is hid with Christ in God. [4] Christ is your life. When He comes, you will be seen with Him in glory.

[5] Put to death all the sins of this world. Sex vices ought to die, and evil thoughts, and passion, and evil desires, and greed for what belongs to others. Greed is one kind of idol worship. [6] These things bring the anger of God upon those who do them. [7] Once you did these things and you lived with people who did them. [8] But now put such things far away from you. Anger, bad temper, ill will, evil talk against people, low dirty stories;—put them all far away from you. [9] Do not lie to one another. You have taken off that old self with its habits like a dirty garment. [10] You have put on the new self. This new self will grow in knowledge of God and will become more and more like Him.

[11] When you have put on this new self, there is no longer any difference between Greeks and Jews, between the circumcised and those who are not circumcised. There is no difference between barbarians and Scythians, or between slaves and free men. Christ is in us all. Christ is all.

[12] You are God's chosen people. He loves you and has made you holy. So you must be tender-hearted, kind, humble, gentle, and patient. [13] Bear with one another. If you have reason to complain against some one, forgive him. The Lord forgave you, so you must forgive others. [14] Above all, love one another. Love makes everything work in perfect harmony. [15] Let the peace of Christ rule in your hearts. Christ has one body and you are its members, so you must work as one. Keep thanking God. [16] Be rich in the words of Christ. Let them live in you. Teach and guide others in wisdom. Sing psalms and hymns and songs of the spirit. Thank God with all your hearts. [17] Whatever you say or do, do it in the name of the Lord Jesus, and give thanks to God your Father through Him.

[18] Wives, obey your husbands. That is the way Christian

wives should live. ¹⁹ Husbands, love your wives, and be kind to them. ²⁰ Children, always obey your parents. That pleases the Lord. ²¹ Fathers, do not make your children angry or they may lose their courage.

²² Slaves, always obey your masters on this earth. Do what they ask whether they are watching you or not. Do it, not just to please them. Do it because you are devoted to the Lord with a sincere heart. ²³ Whatever they give you to do, do it from your heart. Work for the love of the Lord and not just for men. ²⁴ Keep in mind that you are heirs of the Lord, and He will reward you in heaven. You are really slaves of the Lord Christ.

²⁵ Every one who does wrong will suffer for it. God cares nothing about a man's position.

4 Masters, be just and fair to your slaves. Remember that you yourselves have a Master in Heaven.

² Keep praying. Keep thanking God. Keep on the watch.

³ Pray for me, too. I am here in prison because of what I preach. Pray that God may open a door for me to preach the secret truths about Christ. ⁴ Pray that I may tell it clearly as I ought to tell it.

⁵ Be wise in dealing with those who are not Christians. Make good use of every opportunity with them. ⁶ Talk to them kindly. "Season your words with salt," then you will give a good convincing answer to every question.

⁷ My dear brother Tychicus will tell you all about me. He is a faithful minister and my fellow servant in the Lord's work. ⁸ I am sending him to you with this letter. I want him to tell you how we are, and to encourage you. ⁹ I am also sending Onesimus with him. Onesimus is my dear faithful brother. He came from your city. He and Tychicus will tell you everything that has happened to me here. ¹⁰ Aristarchus, my fellow prisoner, sends you his greetings.

And Mark, the cousin of Barnabas, sends his greetings. You have been told about him before. If he comes to see you, make him welcome. [11] Jesus Justus also sends you his greetings. These are the only circumcised men here among my fellow workers for the Kingdom of God. They have been a great comfort to me.

[12] Epaphras, who also comes from your city, sends you his greetings. He is a servant of Jesus Christ. He always remembers you with deep feeling in his prayers. He prays that you may stand up strong like a full grown man in doing God's will. [13] I tell you, brothers, he has a deep concern for you, and for all the other Christians at Laodicea and at Hierapolis.

[14] Luke, the dear physician, sends his greetings, and Demas sends his.

[15] Give my greetings to the brothers at Laodicea. Also give my greetings to Nympha and the church which meets in her house. [16] When this letter has been read to you, I want it read also to the church at Laodicea. I wrote a letter to them, and I want you in Colossae to be sure to read that letter too.

[17] To Archippus I want to say: God gave you a service to perform. See that you do it.

[18] Now I, Paul, write my farewell with my own hand. Remember my prison chains. God bless you all.

Paul
Timothy

PAUL'S FIRST LETTER
TO THE CHRISTIANS IN THESSALONICA

From: *Paul*

To: *The Church in Thessalonica*

1   Silvanus and Timothy join me in writing this letter.

We write to you Thessalonians who belong to God the Father and to the Lord Jesus Christ. Grace and peace be with you.

[2] When we pray we always mention you. We keep thanking God for you. [3] We remember before God our Father your deeds of faith and love. We remember your patience and your hope in our Lord Jesus Christ. [4] Brothers, we are sure that God loves

you and has chosen you. ⁵ Because when we brought you the Good News, the power of the Holy Spirit was behind our words to convince you. You know that while we were there with you, we lived just to do you good. ⁶ You followed the Lord's example and ours. You accepted the word with joy, inspired by the Holy Spirit, even though you had to suffer for it. ⁷ You became an example to all who believe in Christ in Macedonia and in Greece. ⁸ In fact, because of you, the Word of the Lord has been heard not only in Macedonia and Greece, but far beyond. Everywhere the news of your faith in God has spread. We do not need to tell anybody about it. ⁹ People keep talking to us about the welcome you gave us. They talk about the way you gave up your idols to serve the true and living God. ¹⁰ Now you are waiting for God's Son, Jesus. God raised Him from the dead. He is going to come down from heaven and save us from a terrible end.

2 So, brothers, our visit to you certainly did not fail! ² Just before we came to you, Silas and I had been beaten terribly at Philippi—and you know how we suffered. Yet God gave us courage to tell you the Good News in spite of those who fought us.

³ You knew that our message to you was true. Our purpose was pure. We never tried to deceive you. ⁴ God found us fit to be trusted to preach the Good News. So, when we speak, we try not to please men but to please God. He sees what is in our hearts. ⁵ We have never tried to deceive men with false praise —you know that. We have never preached to make money— God knows that. ⁶ We never sought praise from you, nor from any other people. ⁷ As apostles of Christ we have a right to demand honor, but we never did demand it. We were as gentle among you as a nurse taking care of her own children. ⁸ We loved you and desired you for Christ. You were so dear to us that we wanted to give you not only the Good News of God, but also our very souls.

⁹ You remember, brothers, how hard we labored among you. Night and day we worked at our trade to make a living while we were preaching God's Good News to you. We did it so that we would not need to ask you for help. ¹⁰ You and God are witnesses that our life among you who believe was pure and honest and free from blame. ¹¹ You know that we were like a father with his children. We urged you and encouraged you. ¹² We begged each one of you to lead a life worthy of God. We told you how He is calling you into His Kingdom and glory.

¹³ When you heard the word of God from us, you knew that it was more than just a man's words. You received it as really the word of God. That is why we continually thank God about you. The word of God is indeed working in you who believe.

¹⁴ Now, brothers, you have gone through the same trials as the Christian churches in Judea have. Just as they suffered from their fellow countrymen, so you suffered from yours. ¹⁵ The Jews killed the Lord Jesus and their own prophets. They have driven us out. God is pained at them. They are proving themselves to be the enemies of all. ¹⁶ They try to prevent us from preaching to save the Gentiles. They are filling up the measure of their sins. But at last God's anger is coming upon them.

¹⁷ I have been kept away from you, brothers, for a short time. I am separated in body but not in heart. Now I long to see you face to face. I have been very eager to come to you. ¹⁸ I have tried to come. Again and again I have tried to come. But Satan has prevented me from coming. ¹⁹ When the Lord Jesus comes, who do you think will be our hope, our joy, our crown, our pride? Will it be you? ²⁰ Yes! You are our glory; you are our joy.

3 I could no longer bear it not to hear from you. So I decided to stay at Athens alone, ² and I sent Timothy to you. He is my brother and God's servant in preaching the Good News of Christ. I told him to encourage you and make you strong in your faith. ³ I did not want your troubles to cause you to lose heart. You

yourselves know that we Christians must expect to suffer. ⁴ When we were with you we told you that we were sure to be ill-treated. And you see it happened just as we told you. ⁵ That is why, when I could bear it no longer, I sent Timothy to make sure that your faith was holding up. I was afraid that Satan might have tempted you to fall away, and that our labor for you might be lost.

⁶ But Timothy has just come back from his visit to you. He brings me fine news of your faith and love. He says you remember me kindly and that you are very eager to see me again. I, too, am eager to see you. ⁷ So, my brothers, in my sorrow and pain, Timothy's good news about your faith has been a great comfort to me. ⁸ I feel new life in me since I have heard how you stand fast in the Lord. ⁹ How can I thank God enough for you? Thank God for the joy I feel because of you. ¹⁰ Night and day I am praying earnestly that I may see you face to face. I long to help your faith if it lacks anything. ¹¹ May God our Father Himself and our Lord Jesus open the way for us to come to you. ¹² And may the Lord help your love to grow big for one another and for all people. May it become as big as our love for you. ¹³ May God our Father make your hearts strong and holy. May He find you free from every sin when our Lord Jesus comes with all His holy people.

4 I taught you how to live so as to please God. You are living that way now. So, brothers, I beg and pray you, in the name of the Lord Jesus, live that way more and more. ² You know what I told you that the Lord Jesus expects of you ³ God wants you to be holy. So keep away from sex vices. ⁴ Each of you must have his own wife and he must keep his body holy and in honor. ⁵ Do not yield to low sex passions as the Gentiles do who do not know God. ⁶ Let no man wrong his brother in this way, for that would break God's command. The Lord punishes men for such sins, as we have many times warned you before. ⁷ God has not called us to practice vice but to live a holy life. ⁸ The man who refuses to be holy is not opposing men, but God. The

Holy Spirit that God gives you is indeed holy, so we too must be holy.

⁹ I do not need to write to you about loving your brothers. You were taught by God to love one another. ¹⁰ And you do, indeed, love every brother in all Macedonia. I want you, brothers, to show more and more of this love. ¹¹ Aim to live a quiet life and to carry on your own business well. Work with your hands, as I told you to do. ¹² Then you will win the respect of the outside world. And you will not have to depend on any one else.

¹³ Brothers, I want you to know the truth about those who have fallen asleep in death. Do not feel sorry as other people do who have no hope. ¹⁴ We believe that Jesus died and then rose again. So God will bring back to life along with Jesus those who have fallen asleep. ¹⁵ I will tell you what the Lord Himself said about this. He said that we who are alive when He comes shall not be ahead of those who have fallen asleep. ¹⁶ The Lord Himself will come down from Heaven with a shout. The archangel will call. The trumpet of God will sound. Then the dead in Christ shall rise. They shall rise first. ¹⁷ After that we who are still living on earth shall be caught up together with them in the clouds. We shall meet the Lord in the air. Then we shall be with the Lord for ever. ¹⁸ Comfort one another with these words.

5 Brothers, it will do no good to write about the time or the date when this will happen, for no one knows.

² You yourselves well know that the day when the Lord is coming will be like a thief in the night. ³ When people are saying, "Things are very quiet—there is no danger," then sudden destruction will come upon them. It will be like the birth pains of a woman having a child. There will be no escape. ⁴ But you, brothers, are not living in the dark. That day will not surprise you like a thief. ⁵ You are sons of light and of the day. You and I do not belong to the dark or to the night. ⁶ So let us not be asleep as other people are. Let us be awake. Let us not be drunk.

⁷ The dark night is when people sleep, and when drinking men get drunk. ⁸ But we live in the day. So let us be sober and on guard like soldiers. Let us wear Faith and Love to protect our breasts. And to protect our heads let us wear the sure Hope that God will save us. ⁹ For God plans to save us through our Lord Jesus Christ. He does not intend us to suffer from His anger. ¹⁰ Christ died for us so that we may live with Him. Whether we remain awake or fall asleep before He comes, we shall live with Him. ¹¹ So keep encouraging one another. Keep building up one another as you are now doing.

¹² Brothers, I beg you to respect those who are placed over you by the Lord to guide you and work among you. ¹³ Give them high honor and love them because of their work. Live in peace with one another. ¹⁴ I ask you, brothers, to warn those who refuse to work. Encourage those who are afraid. Help the weak. Be patient with every one. ¹⁵ Do not pay back evil with evil. Always seek to do good to one another and to all men. ¹⁶ Be full of joy all the time. ¹⁷ Pray all the time. ¹⁸ Give thanks to God for everything. That is God's will for us who have Christ Jesus. ¹⁹ Do not put out the fire of the Holy Spirit. ²⁰ Do not make light of prophesying. ²¹ Test everything, and hold fast to what is good. ²² But stay away from every form of evil.

²³ It is God who gives you peace. May He make you holy through and through. May your spirit and soul and body all be kept good and true with not a single blame until the Lord Jesus Christ comes.

²⁴ He who calls you will do it, for He is faithful.

²⁵ Brothers, pray for us.

²⁶ Give all the brothers a holy kiss.

²⁷ I request you in the name of the Lord to make sure that all the brothers hear this letter read.

²⁸ The grace of the Lord Jesus Christ be with you all.

Paul
Silvanus
Timothy

132

PAUL'S SECOND LETTER
TO THE CHRISTIANS IN THESSALONICA

From: *Paul and Silvanus and Timothy*

To: *The Church in Thessalonica*

1 We write to you Thessalonians who belong to God our Father and to the Lord Jesus Christ.

² May God the Father and the Lord Jesus Christ give you grace and peace.

³ Brothers, we just have to thank God for you all the time. You deserve it! Your faith in God is growing so great, and your love for one another is increasing. ⁴ We boast about you in the churches of God. We tell people with what a firm faith you endure ill-treatment and suffering. ⁵ The way you take your sufferings proves to everybody that God has judged you worthy of His Kingdom. ⁶ God is just. He will pay back with trouble those who are troubling you. ⁷ To you who suffer, and to us also, God will give His rest when the Lord Jesus comes. The Lord will appear from heaven with His mighty angels in flaming fire. ⁸ He will punish all who refuse to know God and who do not obey the Good News of our Lord Jesus. ⁹ They will be punished with everlasting ruin. They will be put far from the Lord's presence, far from his glorious strength. ¹⁰ But on the day when He the Lord comes, His people will praise Him for His glory. All who have believed in Him will be filled with glad surprise because they believed our message.

¹¹ So we pray for you all the time. We keep praying that God may make you worthy of His call. We pray that by His power He will help you carry out all your good purposes. We pray that you may complete the good work that faith has led you to undertake. ¹² We pray that the name of our Lord Jesus may be glorified in you and you in Him. May every one see the grace of our God and of the Lord Jesus Christ in your deeds.

2 Now, brothers, I will answer your question concerning the time when our Lord Jesus Christ will come, and when we shall gather to meet Him. ² I beg you not to get excited about this question. Do not be too quickly shaken in your minds, even if some one says a spirit told him. I never have written any letter saying that the Lord had already returned. ³ Do not let any one deceive you. That day will not arrive until after a great war, and until after the man-against-law has begun his work. He is going to be destroyed. ⁴ But first he will put himself high above every so-called god and every object of worship. He will seat himself in the temple of God and declare that he is God. ⁵ When I was with you I told you this. Do you not remember? ⁶ I told you what is still holding him back. But he will appear when his time has come. ⁷ He is now doing his evil work in secret. When the one who is holding him back is gone, ⁸ then the man-against-law will come out into the open. But when the Lord Jesus comes He will destroy him with the breath of His mouth and will put an end to his evil work.

⁹ With Satan's power this man-against-law will come. He will show false miracles and false signs and wonders. ¹⁰ He will deceive with evil tricks all those who are on the way to destruction. They too will die because they do not love the truth that could save them. ¹¹ Because they hate the truth, God lets evil powers deceive them so that they believe a lie. ¹² For any one who refuses to believe the truth and who delights in evil, will be condemned.

¹³ But we always have to thank God, brothers, for you who are so dear to Him. You are the first ones whom God chose in Thessalonica. He chose to save you, and to make you holy by His Spirit, as you put your faith in His truth. ¹⁴ When we preached the Good News to you, God called you so that He might give you the glory of our Lord Jesus Christ. ¹⁵ So stand firm, brothers. Hold fast to what we taught you while we were with you, and to what we wrote in our letter.

¹⁶ We told you how much our Lord Jesus Christ and God our

Father loved us. In their loving kindness they have given us great hope, and everlasting comfort. [17] May they fill your hearts with courage and make you strong and sure in every good word and deed.

3   Brothers, pray for us. Pray that the word of God may speed on and win many victories as it did among you. [2] Pray that we may be saved from the hands of evil and wicked men—for not everybody will believe the truth. [3] You can depend on the Lord. He will make you strong. He will guard you from evil. [4] The Lord gives us confidence in you. We are sure that you are doing what we taught you, and we are sure that you will keep on doing it. [5] May the Lord fill your hearts with His love. May He make you strong and faithful in Christ.

[6] Now, brothers, in the name of the Lord Jesus Christ we give you one more charge. Keep away from any brother who leads a lazy life. Such a man is not following the rule which you received from us. [7] We were your example. You well remember that we were not lazy when we were with you. [8] We did not eat any one's bread without paying for it. We worked hard at our trade. We labored night and day so that we would not be a burden to any of you. [9] We had a perfect right to ask you to support us but we did not do it. We wanted to give you a good example to follow. [10] When we were with you, this is the rule which we gave you: "If a man will not work, he shall not eat!" [11] We are told that some of you are not working at your trade, but spend your time talking about other people's affairs. [12] With the authority which the Lord Jesus Christ gave us, we charge and urge such people to work quietly and to earn their own living.

[13] Brothers, never grow tired of doing good.

[14] If any one refuses to obey what we tell you in this letter, mark that man and have nothing to do with him. Then he may feel ashamed of himself. [15] Do not treat him like an enemy, but warn him like a brother.

¹⁶ May the Lord of Peace Himself give you peace always and in every way. And may the Lord be with you all.

¹⁷ I, Paul, write this last greeting with my own hand. This is the way I sign all my letters. It is my handwriting.

The grace of our Lord Jesus Christ be with all of you.

Paul
Silvanus
Timothy

PAUL'S FIRST LETTER
TO TIMOTHY

(From Prison in Rome)

From: *Paul, an apostle of Christ Jesus*

To: *Timothy, my true son in the faith*

1 I was made an apostle of Christ Jesus by the command of God our Savior and of Jesus Christ our hope. ² Timothy, my child, may God our Father and Christ Jesus our Lord give you grace, mercy, and peace of heart.

³ When I was leaving Ephesus to go to Macedonia, I urged you to stay behind. I wanted you to warn certain people not to change what we had taught. ⁴ I wanted you to tell them not to pay any attention to stories that were not true nor to waste their time talking about old family records. Such things only start arguments. They do not build up good order or help our faith in God.

⁵ We should aim to teach love, and a pure heart, and a good conscience, and sincere faith. ⁶ Some people have stopped teaching these things and have gone off after empty arguments. ⁷ They want to be teachers of the law of Moses. But they do not know what they are talking about.

[8] I know that the law is good if we use it right. [9] But the law was not written for good men. It was written for the men who obey no laws and respect no rights. It was written for those who sin and do not worship God. It was written for those who curse God and hate a holy life. It was written for those who kill their own fathers and mothers or other people. [10] It was written for men without morals, for men who practice sex vices against nature, for those who steal children. It was written for those who lie and for those who swear to what is false. It was written for those who do not obey the sound teachings [11] in the Good News of our blessed God.

God has trusted me to preach this glorious Good News. [12] I thank Christ Jesus our Lord for the strength He has given me. He called me to His service, and judged me to be faithful. [13] He had mercy on me although I had cursed Christ and ill-treated His church. He knew that I did these things because I was ignorant and did not believe in Christ. [14] But when the grace of our Lord flowed over me, He gave me a mighty love for Christ Jesus and a mighty faith in Him. [15] One thing I am sure is worthy to be accepted by the whole world: This is that Christ Jesus came into the world to save the wicked. I have been the most wicked of all. [16] I will tell you why I received God's mercy. It was so that Jesus Christ might show His perfect patience toward me, the most wicked of all men. He made me an example of His forgiving love. He showed in me that He will forgive all those who will believe in Him and who will accept everlasting life. [17] Glory be to the King of Ages who lives for ever. To God, whom we cannot see, who is the only God, be honor for ever and ever. Amen!

[18] Now Timothy, my son, I am going to give you your orders. You remember what the prophets told us that you would do. I want you to prove that they were right. Fight the good fight. [19] Hold fast to your faith. Keep your conscience clear.

Some people have stopped listening to their consciences, and their faith has been wrecked. [20] Hymenaeus and Alexander are two men who did this. I handed them over to Satan until they should learn to stop saying awful things against God.

2 These are my instructions to you. First, I urge you to pray earnestly for all men. Plead with God for men, and thank God when He helps them. [2] Pray for kings and all in authority. Pray that they may give us peace and let us live a quiet life, worshiping God and treating all men with respect. [3] This is good and pleasing to God our Savior. [4] He desires all men to be saved and to learn the truth.

[5] There is only one God. And there is only one Man who can bring peace between God and men. He is Christ Jesus. [6] He gave Himself as the price to set all men free from sin. At the right time God sent men out to bear witness to this truth. [7] I am one of those whom He sent to preach this Good News. He sent me to the Gentiles to teach them faith and truth. I am telling the truth and only the truth.

[8] Tell the men of our churches everywhere that I want them to pray. The hands they lift in prayer must be holy. There must be no anger and no quarreling among them.

[9] Tell the women to dress in a fit and proper manner. Tell them to use good sense and good taste. They should not braid their hair or wear gold or pearls or high-priced dresses. [10] Women who profess to be good Christians should be noticed, not for their clothes, but for their good deeds.

[11] A woman must listen quietly in church and she must obey. [12] I do not permit women to teach or to have authority over men. I expect them to keep silent. [13] Adam was made first, and after him Eve. [14] Adam was not deceived by the serpent. It was the woman who was deceived and who first sinned. [15] But let every woman live a humble holy life in faith and love. Then she can be sure God will save her when she bears her children.

3 You hear it said that he who hopes to be a bishop chooses a noble work. That saying is true. ² A bishop must have a good character. He must not be married more than once. He must be sober. He must have good common sense. He must be well-behaved. He must be friendly. He must be a good teacher. ³ Of course he must never get drunk or violent. He must be a gentle man and he must not quarrel. He must not love money. ⁴ He must manage his own family well. He must teach his children to obey and to show respect in every way. ⁵ If a man does not know how to manage his own family, how can he take care of God's church?

⁶ Do not choose as a bishop a man who has only recently become a Christian. He might swell up with pride at this sudden honor and let the devil gain a victory. ⁷ The bishop must be well thought of by people outside the church. If they say evil things about him he is caught in the devil's trap.

⁸ Deacons also must be serious. They must not talk too much. They must not drink much wine. They must not be eager for money. ⁹ They must keep a fast hold on the secret of our faith. Their consciences must be clear. ¹⁰ Test them first, before you make them deacons. If they prove to be free from blame, then let them serve in that office. ¹¹ Their wives too must be serious. They must not say evil things about other people. They must be sober. They must be faithful in all they do.

¹² Deacons must not be married more than once. They must manage their children and their homes well. ¹³ Deacons who do their work well will be respected by others. They will inspire people with confidence in our faith in Christ Jesus.

¹⁴ I hope to come and be with you before long. But I am writing these instructions ¹⁵ because I might be delayed. I want you to know how every one in the family of God ought to behave. God's family is the church of the living God. It is the ground and the base on which we build the truth.

¹⁶ Great, indeed, we confess, is the mystery on which our religion is built. It is the mystery of Jesus.

He appeared in the flesh.
He was approved by the Spirit.
Angels saw Him.
He was preached among the nations.
People all over the world believed in Him.
He was taken up to Heaven in glory.

4 This is the true faith. But the Spirit clearly says that in the future some will fall away from it. They will listen to lying spirits and to the teachings which come from evil spirits. ² People whose consciences are burned with a hot iron are telling these lies. ³ They do not allow marriage. They do not allow people to eat certain foods.

God created every kind of food for us to eat. If we believe and know the truth we may eat them and thank God for them. ⁴ Everything which God created is good. You do not have to refuse to eat anything if you thank God when you eat it. ⁵ It is made holy by the word of God and by your prayer.

⁶ If you help our Christian brothers to understand these things, you will be a good minister of Jesus Christ. Your own soul will be feeding on the teachings of our faith which you have always followed.

⁷ Have nothing to do with those false tales which some people are telling. They are foolish tales and they did not come from God.

Train your soul to live for God. ⁸ To train your body is of some value. But to train your soul to live for God, that is of value in every way. It helps you in this life and also in the life which is to come. ⁹ I am sure that this is a saying worthy to be accepted by everybody. ¹⁰ Because you and I believe it, we continue to work and to suffer. We have set our hope in the living God who is the Savior of all, and especially of those who believe.

¹¹ These then are the things you are to teach and command.

¹² Do not give any one reason to say that you are too young for your office. Be a good example for all who believe in Christ, in your speech and acts, and in your love and faith, and in your pure life. ¹³ Until I come, keep up reading the word of God to the people; and also preach and teach the people. ¹⁴ That was the work which the elders gave you to do when they laid their hands on you and prophesied. Do not neglect it. ¹⁵ Carry out these duties. Devote your time to them. Then every one will see how you are progressing. ¹⁶ Be very careful how you act and what you teach. Keep working hard at your job. If you do that, you will save both yourself and those who hear you.

5 Never lay blame on an older man so as to hurt him. Appeal to him as you would to your father. Treat younger men like brothers. ² Treat older women like mothers, and younger women like sisters. Keep pure in thought and deed.

³ If a widow has no one to support her, the church should take care of her. ⁴ But the children or grandchildren of a widow should be taught their Christian duty to all their family. Teach them that they should help their parents, and so pay back some of what their parents did for them. That pleases God.

⁵ A widow who is all alone in the world puts her trust in God. Night and day she continues to pray and to tell God her needs. ⁶ But if a widow spends her time seeking pleasure, she is dead in spirit even though she is alive in body.

⁷ Here are some rules for you to give, so that the widows may not have a bad name. ⁸ A widow's relatives must care for her. A man who does not provide for a widow who is related to him, especially if she belongs to his own family, denies his faith in Christ. He is worse than a man who does not believe at all.

⁹ Before a widow is put on the church list for aid, she must be over sixty years of age. She must have been married only once. ¹⁰ She must be approved for her good works. She must be a woman who has brought up children. She must have been kind to strangers. She must be a woman who has washed the feet of

God's people. She must be a woman who has tried to help all who suffer. She must have given herself to doing good in every way.

[11] Refuse to put young widows on this church list for aid. For if their natural desires grow stronger than their desire to serve Christ, they will want to marry. [12] Then people will talk against them for breaking their promises. [13] Besides, young widows often learn to be idle. They wander from house to house and get into other people's private affairs. They often tell what they have no right to tell. [14] So I would rather have young widows marry and bear children and take care of their homes. Then our enemies will have no excuse to condemn us. [15] Some widows, I am sorry to say, have already gone over to Satan.

[16] If any believing woman has relatives who are widows, tell her it is her duty to take care of them. Do not let the church be burdened with them. Then the church can care for those older widows who really need help.

[17] Give double honor to those elders of the church who do their duties well. Especially honor those who work hard at both preaching and teaching. [18] And pay them for their work. For our Holy Book says:

"You shall not tie up the mouth of your ox when
it is stamping out the grain with its feet."

And it says:

"The worker deserves his pay."

[19] Never believe a charge made against an elder unless two or three witnesses make the charge against him. [20] If any persons continue to sin, tell them in public that they are guilty; so that other people will be afraid to do wrong.

[21] Timothy, in the sight of God and Christ Jesus and God's chosen angels, I charge you to keep these rules. Keep them without showing favor to one person above another. [22] Do not be in a hurry to lay your hands on a man to make him an elder. Do not have any part in another man's sin. Keep yourself pure.

²³ I am sorry that you are ill so much. Perhaps the water is giving you stomach trouble. Try using a little wine. ²⁴ The sins of some men are plain to see, and soon they are punished. But the sins of others do not come to light until later. ²⁵ That is true also of good deeds. Some are plain for all to see. Some are not plain now, but they cannot stay hid for ever.

6 Tell all slaves to treat their masters with great honor. Then they will not bring reproach on our Christian teaching and on the name of God. ² If a master of slaves believes in Christ, the slaves must not take advantage of the fact that he has now become their brother. They must not stop showing him full respect as a master. Indeed those slaves must serve him even better than they did before. They must love the master whom they serve, because he too believes in Christ.

Now I have told you what you are to teach and preach. ³ If any one is teaching something different, he does not accept the sound words of our Lord Jesus Christ. He denies the teaching which helps us live for God. ⁴ Such a man boasts much, but he really knows nothing. He takes evil pleasure in starting arguments and in fighting a war over words. All this does harm. It causes people to envy, to quarrel, to insult one another, and to think wrong thoughts about one another. ⁵ Men whose minds are evil and who cannot recognize truth, enjoy arguing and fighting about religion.

Many people think religion is a means of making profit. ⁶ The real profit that religion gives is a contented spirit. ⁷ We brought nothing with us into the world, and we can carry nothing away with us when we die. ⁸ So if we Christians have food and clothing, we can be contented. ⁹ But men who desire to be rich are easily tempted to fall into a trap. Their foolish desires lead them into trouble and perhaps into ruin and destruction. ¹⁰ For the love of money is a root of all kinds of evil. Some men were so eager to get rich that they have wandered away from faith in Christ. Then their hearts ached with regret.

[11] But you, man of God, keep far away from all this. Aim to live right, to live for God. Aim to have faith and love and patience. Be a gentle man. [12] Fight the good fight of faith. Take hold of the life that will last for ever. To this good life God called you when you confessed your faith before many witnesses.

[13] When Christ Jesus was before Pontius Pilate, He witnessed without fear to the truth. [14] I charge you also to be true before Christ and before God who gives life to all. Be true to the commands which you received. Keep them without a spot and without reproach until our Lord Jesus Christ appears.

[15] At the proper time Christ will be revealed to us by the blessed and only Ruler, the King of kings and Lord of lords. [16] Only He has lived and will live for ever. He dwells in light which none can approach. No man has ever seen Him or can ever see Him. All honor and power be to Him for ever. Amen.

[17] Tell those who are rich in this world not to be proud of their wealth. Tell them not to put their trust in money. It is easily lost. Tell them to put their faith in the living God who gives us everything that we enjoy. [18] Tell them to use their money to do good. Tell them to be rich in good deeds. Tell them to be generous in sharing what they have with others. [19] Tell them that this is the way they can lay up a treasure in the next life, which is life indeed.

[20] Oh, Timothy, guard what has been put in your care. Keep far away from empty talk and arguments that leave God out. Some people have called this foolish talk "knowledge." [21] But those who believed it have lost their faith.

God bless you!

Paul

PAUL'S SECOND LETTER
TO TIMOTHY

(From Prison in Rome)

From: *Paul, an apostle of Christ Jesus*

To: *My dear child Timothy*

1   God chose me to tell men about his promise. This promise was that they might have life through Christ Jesus.

² Timothy, my child, may God our Father and Christ Jesus our Lord give you grace, mercy, and peace.

³ I am serving the God of my fathers with a clear conscience. I thank God for you, Timothy, and I am always praying for you. ⁴ I never forget your tears the day we parted. I long night and day to see you again, so that I may be filled with joy. ⁵ I remember how deep and real your faith was. Your grandmother Lois and your mother Eunice both had great faith, and now I am sure you have it too.

⁶ I am writing to you to stir up the fire of the Holy Spirit which God gave you when I laid my hands upon you. ⁷ There is no weak fear in the Spirit which God gave us. There is power, and love, and self-control. ⁸ Never be ashamed to witness for our Lord. Never feel ashamed of me here in prison chains. Share with me in suffering for the Good News. God will give us power to endure. ⁹ He saved us, and called us to His holy service. This was not because of any good thing we had done. It was because He had a purpose for us to carry out. Before He made the world, He had planned in His grace to send Christ Jesus to the world. ¹⁰ Now God's purpose has been made clear, for our Savior, Christ Jesus has come. He came and defeated death. Through His Good News He lighted the way for us to everlasting life.

¹¹ I was appointed as an apostle to preach and teach this Good News. ¹² On account of the Good News, I am suffering

here in these chains. But I am not ashamed. I know the God in whom I have put my trust. I am sure that until Jesus comes, He can take good care of the work which I have done for Him.

¹³ Let the sound teaching I gave you be your guide. Be filled with the faith and love which come from Christ Jesus. ¹⁴ Guard the truth which has been put in your care by the Holy Spirit Himself Who dwells in you.

¹⁵ You have heard that the Christians in the province of Asia have turned away from me to another teaching. Phygelus and Hermogenes are two of them.

¹⁶ But Onesiphorus was not ashamed of my prison chains. Many times he has cheered my heart. May the Lord grant mercy to his family. ¹⁷ When he first arrived in Rome, he searched for me everywhere until he found me. ¹⁸ And you yourselves remember all the good work he did while he was in Ephesus. May the Lord show him great mercy on the Day when the Lord appears.

2 Be strong, my son, in the grace which Christ Jesus gives you. ² You heard the things I spoke before many witnesses. Teach all those things to faithful men, so that they will be able to teach others. ³ Share my sufferings like a good soldier of Christ Jesus. ⁴ No soldier, while he is in the service, gets tied up in business. His one aim is to please his commanding officer. ⁵ No man who wins a race receives a crown of victory unless he obeys the rules. ⁶ The farmer who does the hard work, has a right to the first share in the harvest. ⁷ Think about these things, and the Lord will help you to understand what I mean.

⁸ Remember to preach Jesus Christ the son of David, risen from the dead, just as I preached the Good News about Him. ⁹ For this Good News I am suffering and wearing these chains as though I had committed some crime. But never mind—the word of God is not in chains! ¹⁰ I am enduring all this suffering so that God's people may be saved and may receive everlasting glory in Christ Jesus. ¹¹ I am sure that this saying is true:

"If we have died with Him,
we shall also live with Him.

¹² If we endured for Him,
we shall also rule with Him in heaven.
If we deny Him, He will deny us.

¹³ Even though we fail to keep our trust,
He will remain faithful;
He can never deny Himself."

¹⁴ Remind the Christians of this. Charge them before God to avoid arguments about words, for these arguments do no good. They only harm the people who hear them. ¹⁵ Do your best to please God. Aim to be a good workman. Try to handle the message of truth so well that you will never be ashamed.

¹⁶ Avoid empty talk that leaves out God, for it will lead men into ever worse evil. ¹⁷ Such talk eats its way like gangrene. Hymenaeus and Philetus are two of the men who talk like that. ¹⁸ They are not telling the truth for they teach people that the dead have already risen. With such teaching they are overturning the faith of some Christians.

¹⁹ But God's foundation stands firm, and on that foundation are written these words:

"The Lord knows those who belong to Him."

And these words are also written on that foundation:

"Every one who accepts the Lord,
must stop his old bad habits."

²⁰ In any large home there are some vessels made of gold and silver. There are others made of wood and earth. Some are used for high purposes and some for low purposes. ²¹ A Christian is like those vessels. If he washes out his bad habits, he will be holy and fit for the master of the house to use for high purposes.

²² So keep away from the passions of youth. Try to do right. Aim at faith and love and peace. Those who come to God with a pure heart, follow such things.

²³ Keep away also from foolish and ignorant discussions, for you know that they cause only quarrels. ²⁴ A servant of the Lord must not quarrel. He must be kind to every one. He must always be glad to teach. He must be patient. ²⁵ He must be gentle when he corrects those who oppose him. Then, by God's help, they may change their minds and believe the truth. ²⁶ In that way some of those who have been caught by the devil, may escape from his trap.

3 Timothy, you may be sure of this: The last days are going to be very hard. ² Many men will love only themselves. They will love money. They will be proud and vain. They will speak ill of others. They will not obey their parents. They will not be grateful. They will count nothing holy. ³ They will have no mercy. They will refuse any offer of friendship. They will tell lies about people. They will be slaves of passion. They will be cruel. They will hate what is good. ⁴ They will betray their own friends. They will care for nothing and for nobody. Their heads will swell with pride. They will love pleasure instead of loving God. ⁵ They will keep up the forms of religion, but they will deny its power. Stay away from such people. ⁶ Some of them get into private homes and sin with weak women. Those women are loaded with sin themselves and are led about by their own passions. ⁷ Being weak women, they will listen to anybody who comes to them, but they never find the truth.

⁸ Those men with evil minds oppose the truth, just as Jannes and Jambres opposed Moses. Their faith is like false money. ⁹ But they will not get very far. Before long everybody will see that they are false, just as people discovered that Jannes and Jambres were false.

¹⁰ Timothy, you know my teachings. You know how I live. You know my aims, my faith, my patience, my love. You know

that I am faithful. [11] You know how I have been ill-treated and how I have suffered. You know how much I had to endure at Antioch, Iconium, and Lystra. You know how they attacked me and how the Lord delivered me from them all. [12] Everybody who wishes to live for God in Christ Jesus must expect to be ill-treated. [13] Wicked men with their false teachings will continue to grow worse and worse. They will deceive others as they themselves are deceived.

[14] But you, Timothy, hold fast to what you have learned, and to what you are convinced is true. Remember who your teachers were. [15] Ever since you were a child you have known the Holy Writings. There you learned how men are saved by having faith in Christ Jesus. [16] The Holy Writings are inspired by God. They are of great profit for teaching people, for pointing out and correcting their mistakes and for training them to live right. [17] They help the man of God to be prepared and supplied for every good work.

4 Now Timothy, I give you my orders in the presence of God and of Christ Jesus, who will judge the living and the dead. Because Christ and His Kingdom are coming [2] you must preach the word. Keep busy at your preaching in the good season and in the bad season. Convince people, warn them, urge them to accept Christ. Never lose patience, never stop teaching.

[3] The time will come when people will not accept sound teaching. They will gather to hear only the teachers who please their ears and suit their likings. [4] They will stop listening to the truth and turn to strange false stories.

[5] But you, Timothy, must always hold to the truth. Be patient when you suffer. Do your work as a preacher of the Good News and carry out your duties as a minister.

[6] The time for me to leave this life is near. I am soon to be offered as a sacrifice. [7] I have fought the good fight. I have finished the race. I have held fast to the faith. [8] Now the crown for those who love right is waiting for me in heaven. The Lord,

the just judge, will give it to me on that Day. He will reward all of us who have loved Him and who have been eager for His coming.

[9] Do your best to come to me as soon as you can. [10] Demas has left me and gone to Thessalonica. He loves the present world. Crescens has gone to Galatia. Titus has gone to Dalmatia. [11] Only Luke is with me. Get Mark and bring him with you. He is a great help to me. [12] I have sent Tychicus to Ephesus.

[13] When you come, bring my heavy coat. I left it with Carpus at Troas. Also bring the books. Above all, bring me the rolls of parchment paper.

[14] Alexander, the coppersmith, has done me great harm. The Lord will pay him for what he has done. [15] You must be on your guard against him. He has fought against everything I was teaching.

[16] The first time I had to appear before the judge no one came to witness in my favor. They left me all alone. May it not be charged against them. [17] But the Lord was there with me. He gave me strength to make a full statement of the Good News. All the Gentiles in the court heard it. The Lord delivered me out of the lion's mouth. [18] He will save me from every evil and will bring me safe to His Kingdom in heaven. Glory be to Him for ever and ever. Amen.

[19] Give my greetings to Prisca and Aquila and to the family of Onesiphorus.

[20] Erastus has remained in Corinth. I left Trophimus ill at Miletus.

[21] Do your best to come to me here before winter.

Eubulus sends his greetings to you and so do Pudens and Limus and Claudia and all the brothers.

[22] The Lord be with your spirit.

God bless you!

Paul

PAUL'S LETTER
TO TITUS

From: *Paul, a servant of God and an apostle of Jesus Christ*

To: *Titus, my true child in our faith*

1 God has sent me to those whom He has chosen to be His own. I am helping their faith to be strong. I am helping them to know the truth and to do God's will. ² We hope for everlasting life, because God promised it ages ago and He never lies. ³ When the right time came, He revealed His purpose to us. God our Savior commanded me to preach this Good News.

⁴ Titus, my son, may God the Father and Christ Jesus our Savior give you grace and peace.

⁵ I left you there in Crete, Titus, so that you might put everything in good order. I directed you to appoint elders in each town. ⁶ The elders must be men with a clear record. They must be married only once. Their children must believe in Christ. They must not be the kind of children whom people could accuse of fast living or lawbreaking.

⁷ A bishop is the manager of God's work, so he must have a clear record. He must not be proud. He must not have a quick temper. He must not be a man who drinks much wine. He must not be violent. He must not be in love with money. ⁸ He must love to entertain people in his home. He must love what is good. He must be complete master of himself. He must be just. He must be holy. He must be self-controlled. ⁹ He must keep a firm hold on the truth which I taught you. Then his teaching will be sound, and he will be able to silence those who oppose the truth.

¹⁰ I regret that there are many who refuse to obey what I taught them. They are deceiving people with their empty talk. I mean especially those who require people to be circumcised. ¹¹ Their mouths must be stopped, for they are destroying the

faith of whole families. Just to get money, they teach what they have no right to teach.

[12] One of their own prophets in Crete said, "Cretans are always telling lies. They are wicked, lazy beasts. They live only for their stomachs."

[13] He told the truth. So be firm in telling them their mistakes. Make their faith sound. [14] Do not let them listen to false tales which some Jews are telling them. Do not let them follow any rules made by men who will not believe the truth. [15] Teach our Christians that all things are pure when their hearts are pure. But nothing is pure to men without faith, for their hearts are evil. Their thoughts and their consciences are foul and dirty. [16] They pretend that they know God, but their deeds prove that they do not know Him. Their actions are disgusting. They break God's laws. They are not fit for any kind of good work.

2 Titus, what you teach must be sound. [2] Tell older men not to drink much wine. Tell them to be serious. Tell them to practice good sense. Tell them to be sound in their faith. Tell them to love their brothers and to be faithful to Christ.

[3] Tell the older women to honor God by what they do. They must not say anything to hurt other people's reputations. They must not be slaves to drink. They must teach only what is good. [4] They must train the younger women to love their husbands and their children. [5] They must teach them to practice good sense, and to have good morals. They must teach them to be good wives and good mothers, and to be kind. They must teach them to carry out the wishes of their husbands. Then these young women will give other people no reason to talk against our religion.

[6] Urge the young men to practice self-control. [7] You, yourself, must be an example of the good life in every way. Be honest and serious when you teach. [8] Be so sound in what you say that no one can deny it. Then any one who opposes you will be put

to shame. He will not be able to find anything bad to say against you.

⁹ Tell slaves to obey their masters and to please them in every way. Christian slaves must never be rude. ¹⁰ They must not steal. They must show every day that they are truly faithful. Then they will bring honor to the teachings of God our Savior. ¹¹ God, in His grace, sent Christ to save all men. ¹² Christ taught us not to leave God out of our lives. And he taught us to give up the passions of this world. He told us to live a good life of self-control and to obey God, while we are in this world. He taught us to use good sense. ¹³ Now we are waiting in the blessed hope that our great God and Savior Jesus Christ will appear in His glory. ¹⁴ Christ gave Himself on the cross to purchase us all from our sins and to make us pure. He wants us to be His very own people, filled with His zeal to do good. ¹⁵ Tell this to the Christians. Encourage them, and correct them. You have full authority, and every member of the church must respect it.

3 Remind Christians to submit to the men who rule over them. Tell them to obey those in authority. Tell them to be ready to do any kind of honest work. ² Tell them not to speak evil of any one. Tell them not to quarrel. Tell them to be gentle and very polite toward all men.

³ All of us were at one time foolish. We did not obey God. We had been led into evil lives. We were slaves of all kinds of passions and evil pleasures. Our days were full of ill will and envy. Men hated us and we hated them. ⁴ Then the good God our Savior came and brought us His loving kindness. ⁵ He saved us from our evil lives. We had done nothing to deserve His kindness, but He had mercy on us and washed away our sins. We were born again with a new life through the Holy Spirit. ⁶ Upon us God poured His glorious Holy Spirit through Jesus Christ our Savior. ⁷ In His grace He forgave all our sins. Now we are heirs of eternal life.

⁸ All this is true and I want you to teach it over and over

again. Tell those who believe in God that they must take care to do useful work. This is what helps and blesses people. ⁹ Tell them to avoid foolish arguments about family records. Tell them not to argue and quarrel about questions of the law. Such talk only wastes their time. It is of no profit to anybody. ¹⁰ If any man tries to divide our people, warn him once, warn him twice. If he does not then stop quarreling have nothing more to do with him. ¹¹ A man like that has a twisted mind, he is full of sin, and he condemns himself.

¹² I plan to send either Artemas or Tychicus to you. When he arrives do your best to come to me at Nicopolis, where I have decided to spend the winter. ¹³ When Zenas, the lawyer, and Apollos go on their journey, do all you can to help them on their way. See that they have everything they need.

¹⁴ Tell our Christian people to learn to earn their living by doing honest work. Then they will be able to help people who are in need. They will not be like the kind of trees which bear no fruit.

¹⁵ All the Christians who are here with me send you their greetings. Please greet all the Christians there who love us because their faith and ours is the same.

God bless you all!

Paul

THE LETTER PAUL WROTE
TO PHILEMON
(From Prison in Rome)

From: *Paul, a prisoner for Jesus Christ, and brother Timothy*

To: *My dear fellow worker Philemon*

² And to our sister Apphia, and to our fellow soldier Archippus, and to the church which meets in your house.

³ May our Father God and our Lord Jesus Christ give you grace and peace.

⁴ I always thank God when I am praying for you. ⁵ I have heard how you love all of God's people, and I have heard about your faith in our Lord Jesus Christ. ⁶ I pray that every one who meets you may catch your faith and learn from you how wonderful it is to live in Christ.

⁷ My brother, your love has given me great joy and comfort. You have filled the hearts of God's people with new zeal.

⁸ There is one thing which I believe you ought to do for Christ. I would not hesitate to tell you what it is. ⁹ But because I love you and you love me I would rather appeal to your heart.

So now I, Paul, an old man in prison for Christ Jesus, ¹⁰ appeal to you for my child Onesimus. (I have become his father here in prison.) ¹¹ Although his name "Onesimus" means "useful," he was very far from useful to you before he found Christ! But now he is entirely changed. Now he will be very useful to you, as he is useful to me here in prison. ¹² As I send him back to you, I am sending my own heart. ¹³ I wanted so much to keep him here with me to serve me as you would like to serve me, while I lie in prison for the Good News. ¹⁴ But I did not want to keep him without your consent. If you send him back to me, I want it to be of your own free will. I did not want to seem to press you.

¹⁵ For you may want to keep Onesimus. God may have planned that he should be parted from you for a while, so that you could have him back for a lifetime.

¹⁶ I hope you will receive him, no longer as a slave, but as a dear brother. I love him greatly. How much more will you love him, both as a man and as a fellow Christian!

¹⁷ I appeal to you as my brother in the faith, to receive Onesimus as you would receive me. ¹⁸ If he ever wronged you, or if he owes you anything, charge it to my account.

¹⁹ I, Paul, write this with my own hand. I will pay it back. Besides, you owe me your very self! You know that this is true without my saying it.

²⁰ Yes, brother, now you can be "Onesimus" ("useful") to me in the Lord. Make my heart glad in Christ.

²¹ As I write this letter to you, I feel sure that you will do, not only what I have suggested, but even more than I have asked.

²² Will you also please get a room ready for me? I am hoping that by your prayers I shall be set free and be able to come back to you.

²³ Epaphras, my fellow prisoner in Christ Jesus, sends you his best wishes. ²⁴ So do Mark, Aristarchus, Demas, and Luke, my fellow workers.

²⁵ May the grace of the Lord Jesus Christ be with your spirit.

Paul
Timothy

A LETTER
TO JEWISH CHRISTIANS

Dear Brothers in Christ:

1 God has spoken in many different ways. In old times He spoke to our fathers through the prophets. ² But in these last days He has spoken to us through His Son. He appointed His Son as the heir of everything God made. Indeed it was through His Son that God created the world. ³ The Son has revealed to us God's glory. He is a perfect model of God's nature. He holds up the whole created world by the power of His word.

The Son made a way for us to be clean from sin. When He had done that, He sat down at the right hand of the Lord God on high.

⁴ The Son of God is far superior to the angels, and His name is far above theirs. ⁵ God never told an angel:

> "You are my Son;
> today I have become your father."

God never said about any angel,

> "I will be a Father to him,
> and he shall be my son."

⁶ But when God brought His first-born Son Jesus, into the world, He said:

> "Let all the angels of God worship Him."

⁷ God never called the angels sons; He called them servants. The Holy Writings say:

> "He makes his angels winds;
> He makes these servants of His into flames of fire."

157

⁸ But this is what God says to His Son:

> "You shall sit on the throne of God for ever,
> you are just and perfect in ruling your kingdom.
> ⁹ You have loved right and hated wrong.
> Therefore your God has poured
> more of the oil of joy upon your head
> than on the heads of all your companions."

¹⁰ And again God says to His Son:

> "You, O Lord, laid the foundation
> of the earth at the very beginning,
> and the heavens are the work of Your hands.
> ¹¹ They will be destroyed
> but You will remain.
> They will grow old like clothing;
>
> ¹² You will roll up the heavens like a robe;
> they will be changed like a coat.
> But You are ever the same,
> and Your years will never end."

¹³ God never said to any angel:

> "Sit at my right hand
> until I make your enemies
> into a footrest for your feet."

¹⁴ No, the angels are only spirits who serve God. He sends them out to help the people who are going to be saved.

2 We must pay close attention to the message we have heard, for fear we may lose it. ² The message which the angels declared proved to be true. Every sin and every failure to obey that message was punished. ³ How then can we escape punishment if we neglect God's great offer to save us?

The Lord Himself first gave the message. Those who heard

158

Him told us that it was true. ⁴ God also proved that it was true by working signs and wonders and miracles. And He proves it to each one of us now by giving us His Holy Spirit.

⁵ We have said that the world to come is not going to be under the rule of angels. It will be under the rule of God's Son.

⁶ Here is another passage which we need to study carefully:

"What is man that you think so much of Him?
Who is the Son of Man that you love Him so much?

⁷ "For a little while you made Him lower than the
    angels.
Then you crowned Him with glory and honor.
You have put Him in charge of everything you
    ever made.
⁸ You have put everything under His feet."

Do these words "under His feet" refer to all of us human beings? Does it mean that nothing is outside the control of the human race? No, we can see that many things are not yet under our control. ⁹ But we see that these words do apply to the One Man, Jesus. All things are now coming under His control. He was made "lower than the angels" for a little while. That was because God had pity on us, and gave Jesus to suffer on the cross in order to taste death for us all. But after that, God "crowned Him with glory and honor."

¹⁰ All things were made by God and for God's purpose. His purpose was to bring many men as His sons, to glory. To carry out His purpose, God made His Son Jesus perfect through suffering. This was proper because, by suffering for us, Jesus was able to save us. ¹¹ Jesus makes us holy.

We and Jesus are children of the same Father! That is why Jesus is not ashamed to call us His brothers. ¹² He says to His Father:

"I will tell Your name to my brothers,
    in the church I will sing Your praises to them."

159

¹³ In another place the Son says,

"In God I trust."

And again He says:

"Here I am,
and here are the children whom God gave me."

¹⁴ Just as it is true that we and Jesus have the same Father, it is also true that we have the same flesh and blood. Jesus took our nature. He died as we die, so that He might destroy the devil, who is the king of death. ¹⁵ He set us free from death. We need no longer be slaves to the fear of death.

¹⁶ Jesus was not setting angels free from death. He was setting men free, men like us sons of Abraham. ¹⁷ Before He could do this, He had to be made a man exactly like us, and we were His brothers. As our brother He could become our high priest. Then as a faithful high priest, He could have mercy on us. As our high priest He could make a sacrifice of Himself that would wash away our sins.

¹⁸ He suffered as we do. He was tempted as we are. That is why He is able to understand us and to help us when we are tempted.

3 So, holy brothers, let us look upon Jesus as the high priest of our religion. He was sent by God to call you to share the kingdom of heaven.

² Jesus was faithful to God, who gave Him His work to do, just as Moses was faithful in God's house. ³ But there is a vast difference between them. God considered Jesus Christ worthy of far greater glory than Moses. He who builds a house has more honor than the house. ⁴ Every house has to be built by some one. The one who built the whole created world was God through His Son Christ. ⁵ In God's house, Moses was only a servant—a faithful servant. Moses in his day spoke things which God made clear to men a long time later. ⁶ But Christ is far

more than God's servant. He is the faithful Son whom God trusts to rule His "house." We ourselves are the "house of God where Christ must rule." This wonderful truth is our glory and our hope. We must hold fast to that hope to the end. ⁷ For the Holy Spirit warns us:

> "Today, when your hear His voice
> ⁸ do not let your hearts grow hard,
> as your fathers did when they turned against Me,
> in the days when they tried My patience in the desert.
> ⁹ Your fathers tried My patience every day,
> though they saw how I worked for them for forty
>   years.
> ¹⁰ I became angry with your fathers.
> I said: 'Their thoughts are always wrong.
> They never understand what I am doing for them.'
> ¹¹ I was angry at them, and I swore
> that they should never enter into My Rest."

¹² Take care then, brothers, that none of you have hard evil hearts which refuse to believe and so fall away from the living God. ¹³ Warn one another every day, while it is still "today," for fear any of you be deceived by sin and let your hearts grow hard. ¹⁴ For we will share Christ's Kingdom, only if we hold fast to our first faith to the end. ¹⁵ The Holy Writings say,

> "Today, when you hear His voice,
> do not let your hearts grow hard,
> as your fathers did when they turned against Me."

¹⁶ Who were those men who heard God's voice but turned against Him? They were our own fathers after they left Egypt under Moses. ¹⁷ Who made God angry for forty years? It was those of our fathers who sinned. They fell dead in the desert. ¹⁸ Because they did not obey God, He swore that they should never enter His Rest. ¹⁹ You see that they were kept out of His Rest because they did not believe.

4 Today God offers us the same chance to enter His Rest. We must watch out for fear that some of us may fail to enter. ² We have the same Good News that came to our fathers. But it did them no good because they did not believe it. ³ It is only because we have believed that we enter God's Rest. God said of our fathers:

> "I swore in My anger
> that they should never enter My Rest."

God had that Rest ready for those who love Him even before He created the world. ⁴ Somewhere our Holy Writings speak of God's seventh day of Rest in these words:

> "On the seventh day God rested from all His work."

⁵ But God said of those who turned against Him,

> "They shall never enter My Rest."

⁶ As I said before, He had given them the Good News and a chance to enter His Rest; but they had not obeyed Him and so they did not enter it. But He still has that same Rest ready for some of them to enter. ⁷ Again He sets a time. He says, "Today is the time." God said this through David a long time after the days of Moses. His words again were:

> "Today, when you hear His voice,
> do not let your hearts get hard."

⁸ It is clear that Joshua did not lead our fathers to "God's Rest." If he had, God would not have spoken of another "today" a long time after that. ⁹ Yes, today is the day when God's Sabbath Rest is again waiting for His people. ¹⁰ If we enter it, we shall rest from our work just as God rested from His. ¹¹ Let us try hard to enter. Let none of us fail by refusing to obey, as our fathers did.

¹² The word of God is alive and active. It is sharper than a two-edged sword. It cuts straight down and divides the soul from

the spirit. It cuts through the joints and the center of the bones. His word judges even our thoughts and our intentions. [13] Nothing can be hidden from God. Everything is bare and open to the eyes of the God with Whom we have to deal.

[14] But we have a great high priest, and He has gone up to heaven. He is Jesus the Son of God. So let us hold on to our faith in Him. [15] Our high priest has great sympathy for us. He knows how weak we are. He was tempted in every way as we are, but He never sinned. [16] So we dare to come to God's throne with confidence in His forgiving love. There we shall receive God's mercy, and His grace will help us whenever we need help.

5 High priests are always chosen from among the people. A high priest represents his fellow men before God. He offers gifts and sacrifices for sins. [2] A high priest knows how to be gentle with the ignorant and with those who go wrong, for he is just a weak man himself. [3] In fact, he has to offer sacrifices for his own sins as well as for the sins of his people.

[4] A high priest does not elect himself to that position. He must be called by God, just as Aaron was. [5] Even Christ did not make Himself our high priest. He was appointed by God. God said to Him:

> "You are My Son;
> today I have become Your Father."

[6] And in another place God said:

> "You are a priest for ever
> after the order of Melchizedek."

[7] While Jesus was here in the world in His flesh, He offered up many prayers and requests to God. With tears and loud cries He called upon God who was able to save Him from death. God heard Him because He loved and honored God. [8] Even though He was God's Son, Jesus learned through suffering what it means to obey God's will. [9] When that suffering had made Him perfect,

163

He became the One who could save those who obey Him. He gives them eternal life.

[10] God made Jesus High Priest

"after the order of Melchizedek."

[11] I have much to say about this. But I find it hard to make clear to you because your hearing has become so dull.

[12] By this time you ought to know enough to be teachers. Yet you still need to be taught the first simple truths of God's word. You still need milk, not solid food. [13] Any one who lives only on milk is a child and he cannot understand the deeper moral truth. [14] Solid food is for those who have grown-up. It is for those who have trained their minds by long practice to know good from evil.

6 Let us now go beyond those first simple children's teachings about Christ. Let us go on to the higher truths which are for grown-up men and women. We do not need to go back and lay the first foundations again. You already know the simple truths like these:

We must repent for our evil deeds.
We must put our faith in God.
[2] We must be baptized.
We may lay our hands on people and bless them.
The dead shall rise.
The judgment day is coming.

Those are all simple truths. [3] Now we will go on to higher truths, if God is willing.

[4] Some who were once Christians have lost their faith. They once saw the true light. They tasted the gifts from heaven, and they received the Holy Spirit. [5] They found that God's word is good. They saw that Divine Power Which will rule in the ages

to come. [6] Those who fall away after all that, are nailing the Son of God to the cross once more. They are holding Him up to public shame. It is impossible to bring such people back to God, for they will not repent.

[7] God treats people as He does the soil. If the soil drinks the rain and produces plants that are good for food, God blesses that ground. [8] But if the ground produces only thorns and weeds, it is not worth anything. It will be cursed and burned like a desert.

[9] What I have just said, dear friends, does not apply to you. I feel sure that you are going to bear good fruits and so be saved. [10] God is always fair and just. He does not forget your good work and your love. He remembers every kind thing that you have done and all that you are still doing for His people. [11] Keep the zeal and the hope you now have in Christ, until the very end. [12] Do not get lazy. Imitate those who were faithful to death. They have now gone to heaven as heirs of God's promises.

[13] When God made his great promise to Abraham, He swore by Himself. (There was nothing higher than Himself that He could swear by.)

[14] God swore to Abraham:

"Surely I will bless you,
and surely I will give you a vast number of children."

[15] Abraham waited with patience, and God gave him just what He had promised.

[16] In this world when men take oaths, they usually swear by something greater than themselves. That is one way they end their arguments. [17] God wanted to make Abraham feel perfectly sure that God would never change His mind, so He took an oath. [18] God's promise cannot fail and His oath can never change. God cannot prove false. That is why we who go to Him to be saved can put perfect confidence in His promises. Let us hold fast to the hope which God has offered us. [19] This hope is a strong sure anchor for our souls. With this hope we can

enter even the holy place inside the temple curtain. [20] This is where Jesus has gone to prepare the way for us.

Jesus has become our High Priest for ever, like Melchizedek.

7 Now I will explain to you why I have compared Christ to Melchizedek. In the days of Abraham, Melchizedek was the king of Salem. He was a priest of the most high God. When Abraham defeated a number of kings and was returning home, Melchizedek met him and blessed him. [2] Then Abraham paid Melchizedek one tenth of all he had taken from the kings.

The word "Melchizedek" means "King of what is right." He was the king of Salem. The word "Salem" means "Peace," so Melchizedek, "King of what is right," was also the "King of Peace."

[3] Melchizedek had neither father nor mother. He had no family connections at all. He had no beginning and no end. He was and is for ever a priest, like the Son of God.

[4] Now we see what a great man Melchizedek was! Abraham paid him one tenth of all he had taken in battle. [5] The Jewish law tells the priests of the family of Levi to take one tenth of the income of the people. Our priests are taking this tenth from their own brothers, for all of them alike are children of Abraham. [6] But this man, Melchizedek, was not like our priests, for he did not belong to the family of Levi. Yet Abraham gave him a tenth part of his goods. And Melchizedek blessed Abraham, although Abraham had already received God's wonderful promise. [7] It is the greater person who always blesses the one below him. So Melchizedek must have been even greater than Abraham.

I will tell you why he was greater. [8] The Jewish priests, who take the tenth are only men and they will die. But our sacred writings say that Melchizedek will never die and is still alive. [9] One might even say that Levi himself paid a tenth to Melchizedek, [10] for Levi was at that time a seed in the body of Abraham. So you see how great Melchizedek was!

[11] Our fathers received the law at the time when Levi and his sons were priests. But those priests could not make the people perfect nor free them from sin. A better priest was needed who could do what these sons of Aaron and Levi could not do. We needed a Priest from the line of Melchizedek. And that Priest did come from Melchizedek's line—He was Jesus Christ.

[12] If Christ came from a new line of priests, that means the law regarding priests has been changed! That law said that all priests must come from the tribe of Levi. [13] But Christ came from another tribe that never had a priest at the altar. [14] For it is certain that our Lord Jesus Christ came from the tribe of Judah. Moses never said that priests could come from that tribe. [15] So it is plain that this new priest, Christ, came the way Melchizedek came. [16] He came as a Priest, not by belonging to the tribe of Levi, as the law required. He came as Priest by the power of His own eternal life with God. [17] This is what the Holy Book said to Christ:

> "You are a Priest for ever
> after the order of Melchizedek."

[18] We see, then, that God has set aside the commands of Moses. They were of no use because we men were too weak to obey them. That is why the law of Moses could not make anybody perfect. [19] So we see that in Christ, God has given us a far better hope than those priests could offer. For Christ leads us up to God.

[20] And I will tell you another difference between Christ and Levi's sons. God took an oath when he sent Christ. [21] But God never took an oath when the priests of Levi's line took their office. When God made Christ a Priest, here is the oath God took:

> "The Lord has taken an oath
> and will not change His mind:
> 'Thou art a Priest for ever.'"

22 This oath shows us that Jesus has a far better promise from God than the other priests had.

23 I will tell you still another difference between Jesus and the other priests. Those priests had to be many in number because they kept dying off and new priests had to take their place. 24 But Jesus never dies; He is the Priest in heaven for ever. 25 This is why Jesus is able now and for all time to save those who draw near to God through Him. He always lives in heaven and is praying for them.

26 This is the kind of High Priest we needed. He is holy; He is free from blame or spot or sin of any kind; He has been taken up beside God high above the heavens. 27 Every day the other high priests had to offer sacrifices. They offered them first for their own sins and then for the sins of the people. But Jesus had no sin. He did not need to offer sacrifices every day over and over. He sacrificed Himself once and that was enough for all time.

28 The law of Moses appoints weak men, who sin like the rest of us, to be high priests. But after that law had been given, God did something far better. By an oath He appointed His Own Son to be a perfect High Priest for ever.

8 What all this means for us is this: We have such a High Priest seated at the right hand of God in heaven. 2 He is the minister of that Holy Place. There in heaven is the true place of worship. God set it up, not man.

3 Every high priest here on earth is appointed to offer gifts and sacrifices. So Christ also must offer something in heaven. 4 If He lived here on earth, He would not be a priest at all. For there are enough priests already who make the kind of offering that Moses' law requires. 5 The sacrifices which these priests on earth offer are only a copy or a shadow of Christ's sacrifice in heaven. When Moses was ready to put up the tent of sacrifice at the foot of Mt. Sinai, God said to him:

"Be sure to make it like the pattern in heaven, which I showed you when you were on Mount Sinai."

⁶ So, I repeat, Christ's service as Priest in heaven is far superior to the service of priests on earth. The agreement which made Christ our High Priest, is far superior, because in it God promised much better things than He promised through Moses. ⁷ If the first agreement had been all right, there would have been no need for another one. ⁸ But God Himself found fault with the people who lived under that old agreement, and He promised a better one:

> "The day will come," says the Lord,
> "When I will make a new agreement
> with the house of Israel and with the house of Judah.
> ⁹ It will not be like the one which I made with their fathers.
> On that day I took their fathers' hand
> to lead them out of Egypt.
> But they did not keep their agreement with me,
> And so I did not listen when they called,"
> says the Lord.

> ¹⁰ "But I will make this new agreement
> with the children of Israel.
> When that day comes," says the Lord,
> "I will put My laws into their minds,
> and I will write them in their hearts.
> I will be their God
> and they shall be My people.

> ¹¹ "They will not need to teach their neighbors
> or their brothers about the Lord,
> for they shall all know Me.
> The humble people and the great shall know Me,

¹² "I will have mercy on them for their wicked deeds.
And I will not remember their sins any more."

¹³ When God speaks of a new agreement He shows that the old agreement with Moses is out of date. And what is old and out of date is ready to disappear entirely.

9 Now we will consider the differences between the old agreement and the new. The old agreement had its rules for worship. It also had a Holy Place on this earth.

² Moses built two tents. The front tent is called the "Holy Place." In this tent was the lampstand and the table and what they called "the bread of the Presence." ³ Behind a curtain in the rear of this tent was the second tent. It was called "The Holy of Holies." ⁴ In this "Holy of Holies" were an altar to burn incense, and a large box called the "Ark of the Agreement." Both of these were covered with gold. Inside the Ark were these objects:

> The jar of gold with manna in it,
> Aaron's rod which once budded, and
> the tables of stone, on which God had written His
> agreement.

⁵ The top of the ark was called "God's Mercy Seat." Two glorious creatures (called "Cherubim"), with wings like birds, stood over this "Mercy Seat" so that their wings threw a shadow over it. I must not take any more time to describe these things.

⁶ Into the front tent called the "Holy Place" all the priests could go at any time to perform their worship. ⁷ But they could not enter the tent behind this one, the tent called the "Holy of Holies." Only the high priest could enter that second tent, and he could go in only once a year. When he entered, he had to carry blood with him, and offer it to God for the sins of himself and of the people.

170

⁸ The Holy Spirit helps us see the deeper meaning of these two tents. We can see that the way into the second tent, "The Holy of Holies," is not open to us as long as the first tent is still standing. ⁹ That first tent represents this present age under the law of Moses. Under that law, the priests offer gifts and sacrifices, but these are not able to help the people to worship with a clean conscience. ¹⁰ Their rules all deal with food and drink and washings. They are rules to make their bodies clean—not their souls. They were in force until Christ came to bring in the new order.

¹¹ But now Christ has come as High Priest of the good things which God promised. He went into the perfect "Tent" in heaven. That Tent was not made with human hands, and it does not belong to this world. ¹² He entered one single time into the "Holy Place" where God is. He did not carry the blood of goats or calves with Him. He offered His own blood. That single sacrifice of Himself was enough to save us for ever.

¹³ When people broke the old rules about food and drink and washing, their bodies were called "unclean." Then the priests would sprinkle the bodies of the people with the blood of goats and bulls, or with the ashes of burned young cows. That was to make them "clean" again; but it did not make their consciences clean. ¹⁴ But Christ, through the Eternal Spirit, did far more than that. He offered His Own perfect Self to God. His blood makes our consciences clean from our wicked past. Now we can come and worship the living God.

¹⁵ Christ by His death sealed the new agreement between us and God. Christ's death pays the price to deliver us from the sins which we committed under the old agreement. That is the reason that we whom He has called will be heirs of eternal life.

¹⁶ We can understand this better by comparing it to the wills which men make. When a man makes a will, people do not put that will into effect until the man is dead. ¹⁷ The will has no effect so long as the man who made it is alive. ¹⁸ God's agreement with men also required a death to put it into effect. It did not go into effect without the blood of a dead animal.

¹⁹ This is how Moses made the agreement. First he told the people every commandment of the law. Then he mixed the blood of calves and goats with water. Then with red wool and hyssop, he sprinkled the blood on the book of the laws and on the people. ²⁰ As he did this, Moses said to the people, "This blood binds you to the agreement which God has made with you."

²¹ Moses also sprinkled blood on the tent and on all the vessels used in worship. ²² According to the law of Moses, almost everything was made pure by blood. Unless blood flowed, sins were not forgiven.

²³ The tents that Moses made and everything in them were only copies of those things in heaven. These things on earth were made clean by sprinkling them with the blood of animals. But the Tent in heaven needed a far higher sacrifice than the blood of animals. ²⁴ For you see, this was heaven itself that Christ was entering, and not just a copy made with human hands. Christ entered heaven itself for us, and stands now before the very face of God, to save us.

²⁵ Christ was not like the high priest down on this earth who enters the "Holy of Holies" once a year to offer blood which is not his own. For Christ gave His own blood as an offering. He did this just once, not many times. ²⁶ He has not suffered and died over and over every year since the world began. He did not need to do that. He has come at the end of the age and sacrificed Himself once for all to put an end to sin.

²⁷ All of us must die once and then we face the judgment. ²⁸ So Christ too gave Himself as a sacrifice only once, to take away the sins of many. When He returns to this earth the next time, He will not sacrifice Himself again. He will come and save all those who are eager and waiting for Him.

10 But the law cannot save us. The law gives us only a shadow here on earth of the good things which are to come. It does not give us those good things. For the sacrifices which the priests offer continually every year, can never make perfect the people who come to worship. ² If those sacrifices could make the souls of the people clean, they would not feel guilty of sin any longer, and they would not need to offer any more sacrifices. ³ But those sacrifices do not remove sin. They only keep reminding the people of their sins year after year. ⁴ It is not possible for the blood of bulls and goats to take away any man's sins.

⁵ This is why, when Christ came down to the world, He said to God,

"You do not want any other sacrifices and offerings,
for you have prepared My body for an offering.
⁶ You take no pleasure in burnt offerings and
sin offerings of animals.
⁷ Then I said, 'I have come to do thy will, O God,'
as the Holy Book said that I would do."

⁸ Look at those words of Christ very carefully. He says to God, "You do not want sacrifices and offerings—you do not want burnt offerings or sin offerings. They have not pleased you." He means the things which are sacrificed under the law of Moses.

⁹ Then He says, "I have come to do Your will." He did God's will when He died on the cross. That is how He has put an end to the old sacrifices and has established a new way to God. ¹⁰ Through that offering, which Jesus Christ made of His own body by God's Will, we have been made holy. He sacrificed His own body once for all time.

¹¹ The priests on earth still stand every day at the altar offering the same kinds of sacrifices over and over. Yet their sacrifices can never take away any sins.

¹² Christ offered only one sacrifice for sin and that was enough for ever. Then He went and sat down at the right hand of God. ¹³ He is waiting there "until His enemies are made a footrest for His feet." ¹⁴ So with that one sacrifice He made us holy and brought us into perfect union with God. ¹⁵ The Holy Spirit makes us sure of this. God said,

173

16 "This is the agreement which I will make with them.
    After those days, says the Lord, I will put My
    laws in their hearts
    and write them in their minds."
17 Then God added, "I will not remember their sins and
    their evil deeds any longer."

18 When our sins are forgiven, no more sacrifices are needed.

19 And now, brothers, through the blood which Jesus gave, we enter God's holy place with confidence. 20 We come to God by the new and living way which Christ opened for us through the curtain. He opened that way by sacrificing Himself.

21 Now we have Christ as a great Priest over the house of God. 22 Let us come to Him with an honest heart. Let us come full of confidence, for our hearts have been sprinkled from a bad conscience and our bodies have been washed with pure water. 23 Let us hold fast to our faith. Let nothing shake it. He who made His promises to us, will not fail. 24 Let us think of ways to stir up one another to love and to good deeds. 25 Let us not forget to meet together. Some people are neglecting these meetings. Encourage one another, especially since you see that the Day of the Lord is drawing near.

26 But, brothers, we cannot continue to live in sin after we have learned the truth. If we choose an evil life, there is no sacrifice which can save us. 27 We will have to face the terrible day of judgment, when fierce fires will burn up the enemies of God.

28 Under the old agreement, if any one broke the law of Moses and two or three witnesses condemned him, he died without mercy. 29 What do you think a man deserves today if he stamps his feet on the Son of God? What does he deserve if he treats the blood of God's new agreement like common dirt? What punishment does a man deserve if he insults the Spirit of God who offers him mercy?

³⁰ It was God who said,

"It is I who will punish the wicked.
I will pay them back."

And it was God who said,

"The Lord will judge His people."

³¹ It is an awful thing for a bad man to fall into the hands of the living God.

³² My brothers, you started well. You remember those days just after you heard the truth. Then you had a hard struggle and you endured much suffering. ³³ You were insulted and beaten in public. When your brothers were ill treated, you shared their sufferings. ³⁴ You pitied those who were in prison. When enemies stole your property, you counted it a joy. For you know that you possess something far better which will last for ever.

³⁵ And now do not lose your confidence. For your reward will be great. ³⁶ You must be patient. You must keep on doing God's will. Then He will give you what He promised you. God said,

³⁷ "In a little while the One Whom you expect will come.
He will not be long in coming."

³⁸ "By faith shall the just man live.
But if he draws back,
My soul will take no delight in him."

³⁹ You and I are not among those who are going to draw back and be destroyed. We are among those who will hold on to their faith and save their souls.

11 Faith means being sure of the thing we hope for. It is being convinced of what we cannot see. ² God approved the men of old because they had faith. ³ If we have faith we can understand how the world was created by God's word. By faith we know that God created the world which we see, from things which we cannot see.

⁴ Abel had faith. That is why the sacrifice he offered pleased God more than Cain's sacrifice. Because Abel had faith, God said that his heart was right and accepted his gift. Abel died, yet he is speaking to us even today, because he had faith.

⁵ Enoch had faith. That is why he was taken to heaven without ever dying. Nobody could find his body because God had taken him away. It is written that he pleased God before he was taken up to heaven. ⁶ Unless a man has faith, he cannot please God. Whoever wishes to come to God must believe two things:

First, that God exists, and
second, that He rewards those who seek Him.

⁷ Noah had faith. That is why he listened to what God told him was going to happen. He built an ark to save his family. His faith condemned the lack of faith in all the rest of the world of his day. Noah won the reward that comes to those who are right with God, because Noah had faith.

⁸ Abraham had faith. That is why he obeyed when God told him to leave his home and go to the land which God promised to give him. Abraham went away from home, although he did not know where he was to go. ⁹ Because Abraham had faith, he lived in a foreign land which God had promised should some day be his. He lived in tents. His son Isaac and Isaac's son Jacob also lived in tents. They too had faith that they would be heirs of the land which God promised to Abraham. ¹⁰ Abraham was looking forward to the city of the future, a city with firm foundations. That city was planned and built by God.

¹¹ Sarah had faith. That is why God made her able to have a child long after she was past the age to bear children. God had promised, and she had faith that He would keep His promise.

¹² Abraham was old enough to be dead, yet because he had faith, he became the father of many children. His children be-

came as many as the stars of heaven and the sands on the sea-shore. There were far too many to be counted!

[13] These people of faith never received what had been promised to them, but they died holding on to their faith. They saw the full answer coming far ahead and it made them glad.

They confessed that so long as they lived on the earth they were strangers in a foreign land. [14] People who talk like that show that they are seeking a land that they can call home. [15] They are not talking about the land they have left behind, for they could go back to it if they wished. [16] They desire a better country, a country in heaven. Therefore God is not ashamed to be called their God, for He has prepared for them a City.

[17] Abraham had faith. That is why he was willing to offer up Isaac when God tested him. He got ready to sacrifice his only son, Isaac, at God's command. [18] He was willing to sacrifice Isaac although God had promised him, "Through Isaac your children's children shall continue your name." [19] Abraham believed that God was able to raise men even from the dead. And one may say that God did give back Isaac from death itself.

[20] Isaac had faith. That is why he prayed that Jacob and Esau might have future blessings.

[21] Jacob had faith. That is why, even when he was about to die, he worshiped God, bowing upon his cane, and blessed each of the sons of Joseph.

[22] Joseph had faith. That is why on the last days of his life he declared that the children of Israel would some day leave Egypt. And he told them to bury his bones in their future home in Canaan.

[23] Moses' parents had faith. That is why they were not afraid when the king ordered all baby boys to be killed. Moses' parents hid him for three months, because they saw that he was a beautiful child.

[24] Moses had faith. That is why, when he grew to be a man, he refused to be called a son of Pharaoh's daughter. [25] He preferred to be ill-treated with the people of God, rather than to

enjoy the pleasures of sin for a little while. 26 He thought that any shame suffered for Christ, was worth more than all the treasures of Egypt. He looked to God for his reward. 27 Because Moses had faith, he left Egypt. He was not afraid of the king's anger. He never lost his courage. By faith he saw One coming whom others could not see. 28 Because he had faith, he told all the Hebrews to put blood on their doors, so that the angel of death would pass over their houses without killing their oldest sons. 29 Because Moses had faith, he led the people through the Red Sea as if they were on dry land. But the Egyptians tried to go through the sea and were drowned.

30 Joshua had faith. That is why he marched the people around the walls of Jericho for seven days so that the walls fell down.

31 Rahab the harlot had faith. That is why she gave a friendly welcome to the spies. Because she had faith, she was not killed with the wicked people of Jericho.

32 What more shall I say? I do not have time to tell about the faith of Gideon, and Barak, and Samson, and Jephthah, and David, and Samuel, and the prophets. 33 These men all had faith. And with faith they conquered kingdoms, ruled with justice, and received what God had promised them. Some of them stopped the mouths of lions. 34 Some put out raging fires. Some escaped the edge of the sword. With faith, weak men became strong. They became mighty in battle and put foreign armies to flight.

35 Women had faith, so that their loved ones were raised from the dead.

Many people were tortured but refused to deny God in order to get free. They had faith that when they died they would rise to a better life. 36 Others were insulted or beaten or were chained in prison. 37 They were stoned, they were sawed in two, they were killed with the sword. They went about wearing skins of sheep and goats. They lost all they possessed. They were in hunger and pain and they were ill-treated. 38 They wandered over deserts and mountains and lived in holes and caves of the earth. This world was not worthy of such men.

³⁹ All of them won heaven's praise for their faith. But here on earth they did not receive what God had promised. ⁴⁰ God through Christ had planned something better for us. The work which these men of faith began was not complete without us.

12 These men who died in faith before us are now a great cloud of witnesses surrounding us. So let us lay aside everything that holds us down and the sin that sticks to us so closely. Let us keep on running with all our might the race God gave us to run.

² Let us look to Jesus, for He began our faith and will make it perfect. See how Jesus found His joy in doing God's will! For that joy He suffered on the cross, giving no thought to the shame which He endured. Now He is seated at the right hand of God. ³ Think of the pain He suffered from wicked men. Think how they hated and opposed Him. Then you will not grow tired or lose your courage. ⁴ In your fight with sin, you have not yet had to struggle to the very death. ⁵ Do you remember the warning which God gave you when He called you His sons?

"My son, do not make light of the Lord's discipline.
Do not lose courage when He punishes you.
⁶ For the Lord disciplines every one whom He loves
and uses the rod upon every son whom He accepts."

⁷ So your sufferings are God's discipline. God is treating you as His sons. What son is there whom his father does not discipline? ⁸ If you do not receive discipline, you are not true sons. You are children born out of marriage.

⁹ Our fathers on this earth disciplined us and we respected them. Shall we not be much more willing to submit to the discipline of the Father of our spirits, and so have life? ¹⁰ Our fathers disciplined us for a little while when they wished. But

God disciplines us only for our own good, so that we may become holy as He is holy.

11 It is true that discipline at the time causes pain and is not pleasant. But those who receive God's discipline will produce good fruits. They will be right with God, and they will live in peace.

12 So lift up those discouraged hands which are hanging by your sides. And if you have weak knees make them strong. 13 And be sure to have straight paths to walk in. For if you fall, your weak knees may go out of joint instead of getting well!

14 Try to be at peace with all men. Try to live a holy life. We cannot see God unless we are holy. 15 Be sure that none of you fails to accept God's mercy. Do not let the bitter root of hate grow up among you, for that is what makes trouble and causes many people to sin. 16 Let none of you forget God and fall into vice, as Esau did. As the oldest son, he had a right to be heir to all Isaac had. But for only a dish of food, he was so foolish as to sell his rights as heir. 17 Later when he wanted to be the heir, he was refused although he begged with tears. It was too late then for him to correct his mistake.

18 You and I do not come to worship before a thing which we can touch as our fathers did. They saw the fierce fire on Mount Sinai, and the darkness and the shadows, and the storm. 19 They heard the loud sound of a horn. They heard God's voice from Mt. Sinai, and they begged Moses to ask God to stop speaking. 20 They could not endure the awful command which they heard:

"If even an animal touches Mt. Sinai it shall be stoned."

21 The sight of the mountain was so terrible that Moses said:

"I am trembling with fear."

22 But brothers, you and I have come to Mount Zion, which cannot be seen or touched. We have come to the city of the living God, the Jerusalem of heaven. In this city are thousands upon thousands of angels gathered to praise God. 23 Here too

are gathered the sons of God who were born before our day and who are now citizens of heaven. God, the Judge of all, is there. The spirits of all the just men who ever lived, are there. Now they are perfect in heaven. ²⁴ Jesus, who poured out His blood to seal the new agreement between God and men, is there. That blood which Jesus poured out on the cross to save us, has a meaning far more precious than the blood of Abel had.

²⁵ Be sure, my brothers, that you do not refuse to listen to this message of God. When God gave Moses the law on earth, those who refused to listen did not escape. And we shall not escape if we refuse to listen to God's warning from heaven. ²⁶ At Mt. Sinai His voice shook the earth. But God now says:

> "Only once more I will shake,
> not only the earth,
> but the heavens also."

²⁷ What does God mean when He says "only once more"? He means that this time He will bring the created world to an end. Then only God's Kingdom will remain which can never be shaken.

²⁸ Give thanks, therefore, that we are to receive this Kingdom that can never be shaken. Worship God with holy fear and deep reverence so that He will accept your worship. ²⁹ For our God is a fire that destroys all evil.

13 You must all continue to love one another like brothers. ² Do not fail to be very kind to strangers. Sometimes people have entertained angels without knowing it. ³ Remember those who are in prison as though you were in prison with them. Remember those who are ill-treated, for your body may also suffer.

⁴ You must all hold marriage in very high honor. Keep the marriage bed free from sin. God will punish those who practice sex vice and those who break the marriage promises.

⁵ Keep away from the love of money. Be content with what you have.

God has promised:

"I will never leave you;
I will never forsake you."

⁶ So we can say with confidence:

"The Lord is helping me;
I will not be afraid.
What harm can men do to me?"

⁷ Remember those leaders who spoke the word of God to you, and have gone to heaven. Remember how they lived faithful to the end, and imitate them.

⁸ Jesus Christ is the same today as He was yesterday, and He will be the same for ever.

⁹ Do not let yourselves be carried away by various strange teachings about certain foods. It is by God's grace that our hearts are made strong. Nobody wins God's favor by obeying rules about what food to eat. ¹⁰ We have an altar in heaven from which we can eat the food of the Spirit. The priests who serve their altars on earth may not eat from our Altar in heaven.

¹¹ These priests kill animals and take their blood into the holy place as a sacrifice for sin. Then the bodies of those animals are burned outside the camp or the city. ¹² It was outside the city of Jerusalem that Jesus suffered and died on the cross. There He sacrificed His own blood to make men holy. ¹³ So let us go to Him "outside the gate of the city" and share His shame there.

¹⁴ We Christians have no lasting city of our own on this earth. We are looking for a City that is to come. ¹⁵ So through Jesus, let us every day offer up a sacrifice of praise to God. The fruits which we will offer God will be songs from our lips. Let us never stop singing praises to His name.

¹⁶ Do not forget to help people, and to share what you have with others. That is the kind of sacrifice which gives God joy. ¹⁷ Obey your leaders. Submit to their authority. They keep watch over your souls. They will have to give an account to God

for what they do. Make them feel happy in their work. Do not make them feel sad, for that would be your loss as well as theirs.

18 Pray for us. Our conscience is clear, and we want to be straight and clean in everything we do. 19 Pray especially that I may come back to you soon.

20 Our Lord Jesus Christ is the great Shepherd of the sheep. He sealed the eternal agreement between God and man with His own blood. He died, but the God of peace raised Him from the dead. 21 May God provide you with everything that will help you carry out His will. May He work in you through Jesus Christ so that you may do what pleases Him. Glory be to God for ever and for ever. Amen.

22 I beg of you, brothers, be patient with my words of warning for I have not written a very long letter to you.

23 You will be glad to hear that our brother Timothy is now free. If he comes soon, he and I will visit you together.

24 Give my greetings to all your leaders and to all the people of God. The Christians in Italy greet you.

25 God bless you all.

Writer Unknown

JAMES' LETTER
TO JEWISH CHRISTIANS

From: *James*

To: *The twelve tribes of Israel scattered over the world*

1 I am a servant of God and of the Lord Jesus Christ. I send greetings to you all.

² Be glad, brothers, when you have many trials. ³ You know that trials test your faith and make you firm. ⁴ When you have learned to stand firm in the face of trials your character will be perfect and complete; you will not lack a thing.

⁵ When any one of you needs wisdom, ask God. He is eager to help you and will never find fault with you for making requests. He will give you all the wisdom you need. ⁶ But you must ask in faith. Do not have any doubts about God. The man who doubts is like a wave of the sea. He is blown about by the wind and driven here and there. ⁷ A man like that cannot expect the Lord to give him anything. ⁸ He has two minds and does not himself know what he wants.

⁹ Even a very poor man has reason to be filled with pride and joy because Christ has called him. ¹⁰ And the rich man may be glad even if he loses all for Christ. For rich men will soon pass away like flowers in the grass. ¹¹ The sun rises with its burning heat and the grass dries up. The flowers drop off and their beauty is gone. So the rich man fades away in the middle of his efforts.

¹² Happy is the man who stands firm when he is being tried. If he passes the test he will receive the crown of life which God has promised to those who love Him.

¹³ If a man is tempted he must not say, "I have been tempted

184

by God." God Himself cannot be tempted to do wrong and He does not tempt any one else.

¹⁴ If a man is tempted it is his own desires that tempt him and trap him. ¹⁵ His wrong desires make him imagine evil and give birth to sin. Then when sin is full-grown it gives birth to death. ¹⁶ So, dear brothers, do not let sin deceive you.

¹⁷ Every good thing in us and every perfect gift that we receive is from above. It comes down from the Father of the lights of heaven. But God is not like the sun and the moon which are moving and changing every day. God never changes, and in His light there are no shadows.

¹⁸ God wanted us as His sons. That is why He gave us the truth of the Good News. We are born again. We are God's first fruits. We are the first of all those sons whom God plans to gather from the whole world. ¹⁹ My dear brothers, always keep in mind that you are God's sons.

So let every one of you be ready always to listen, slow to speak, and slow to get angry. ²⁰ When you are angry, you are not living the good life which God demands of His sons. ²¹ Also put away all low morals. Cut out of your life all the weeds of a wicked life. Be humble. Let God plant in your heart the truth which will save your souls.

²² Do whatever God tells you to do. Do not be the kind of men who hear God's message, and then do nothing. Such men deceive themselves but not God. ²³ If any one hears God's message, but does not do it, he is like a man who looks at himself in a mirror ²⁴ and goes away and forgets at once what he looks like.

²⁵ The truly wise man looks into God's law, for that is the only perfect mirror. God's law alone brings true liberty. The wise man obeys this law. He never forgets what he hears, and he always does what he knows is right. That man will be happy in all his work.

²⁶ If any one thinks he is religious but does not control his tongue, he deceives himself. His religion does him no good.

²⁷ There is a kind of religion so pure that God the Father finds no spot in it. It is this: to care for children who have no fathers or mothers; to take care of widows in their trouble; to keep yourself clean from the world's evil ways.

2 My brothers, hold on to the true faith of the Lord Jesus Christ, the Lord of Glory. Show no favors to rich people and do not neglect poor people. ² Suppose a man with gold rings and fine clothing comes into your meeting, and suppose a poor man with dirty clothes comes in. ³ Do not pay special attention to the one who wears the fine clothes. Do not say to him: "Have a seat here, please," while you say to the poor man, "You stand back there," or "Sit at my feet." ⁴ It is all wrong to make such differences between rich and poor. It is all wrong to judge people by their money. ⁵ Listen, my dear brothers. God chose the poor people to be rich in faith. They will be heirs of the kingdom which He has promised to all who love Him. ⁶ Are you going to make these poor people ashamed?

Who are the people who make things hard for you? Who are the people who force you to go to court? They are the rich, not the poor. ⁷ Who are the people who curse the holy name of your Jesus? They are the rich, not the poor.

⁸ Keep the royal law of love which is taught in our Holy Writings:

"Love your neighbor as you love yourself."

Then you will always do right. ⁹ But if you show honor for the rich above the poor, you are committing a sin; you are breaking the royal law of love. ¹⁰ If a man breaks the law of love, he is guilty, even though he keeps all the other laws. ¹¹ Because he who said, "Do not sin with another man's wife," said also, "Do not kill." If you kill, you break the law of love even if you do not sin with another man's wife.

¹² The law of love is true liberty. Speak and act by this law. By this law of love we are going to be judged. ¹³ If you show

186

no mercy for other people, God will judge you without mercy. But if you show mercy, God will judge you with mercy. [14] My brothers, there is no use in a man saying, "I have faith," if he does no loving deeds. That kind of faith cannot save him. [15] Suppose you meet some brothers or sisters who have no clothes or daily food. [16] Suppose you say to them, "Good bye. Don't worry. I hope you will keep warm and find enough to eat." If you give them no help, do you think God will approve of that? [17] Faith is dead if loving deeds do not go with it.

[18] Some one may object: "I thought you said we are saved by faith." Yes, we are saved by faith, but it must be true faith. And loving deeds prove that your faith is true. You may say that you have faith without doing good deeds. But I will prove that my faith is true, by the loving deeds that I do.

[19] You say that you believe that God is the one true God. That is good, but it is not enough. The devils also believe that there is one God, and they tremble with fear.

[20] Foolish fellow, let me prove to you that faith without doing good is empty talk. [21] Take Abraham as an example. Abraham was made right before God by his deeds when he offered Isaac his son upon the altar. [22] His deed, you see, proved that his faith was active and real. His faith was made perfect by his deed. [23] This is why our Holy Writings say:

"Abraham believed God.
    That is why he was counted right with God;
    that is why he was called God's friend."

[24] You see that a man is counted right with God because of his good deeds and not because of his faith alone. [25] In the same way Rahab, the harlot, was counted right because of her loving deed. She received those whom Joshua sent to her country and she helped them to escape; and that kind deed made her right with God.

[26] A body which does not have the breath of life is dead. Just so, faith which does no good works is dead.

3   Brothers, not many of you should be teachers. You know that God will be more severe in judging us teachers than in judging the rest of you.

² All of us make many mistakes. If a man never said the wrong thing, he would be perfect! If a man controls his tongue, he can control every part of his body.

³ We put a bit into a horse's mouth to make him obey us. Then we can guide his whole body. ⁴ Look at a ship! It is big and it is driven by strong winds; yet a man holding a guiding stick can make it go wherever he chooses.

⁵ The tongue is little, but it can make very big boasts. A great forest can be set burning by a very small fire! ⁶ The tongue is a fire. It can do a whole world of evil. It can poison every organ in your body. It can set all nature burning. The fire in the tongue comes out of hell.

⁷ Every kind of beast and bird, every serpent and living thing in the sea can be tamed by men. ⁸ But no man can tame the tongue. It is an evil which never rests and for ever threatens to kill with its poison. ⁹ With the tongue we bless the Lord and Father. And with the same tongue we curse men who are made in the image of God. ¹⁰ From the same mouth come blessing and cursing. We ought not to be like that, my brothers. ¹¹ Does a spring pour fresh water and bitter water out of the same opening? ¹² Can a fig tree ever bear olives? Or can a grape vine ever bear figs? No, and a salt spring can never give fresh water.

¹³ If a man is wise and understanding, he should show it by his good life. Let him be humble and do his work as a wise man would. ¹⁴ Are you bitter or jealous? Is your heart full of selfish ambition? If so, do not boast about your wisdom, for you are not telling the truth. ¹⁵ Do not call those evil things "wisdom from above." They belong to this world; they are from your own lower nature; they are from the devil. ¹⁶ Where people have selfish ambitions and are jealous of one another, there will be all kinds of quarreling and fighting and wicked deeds.

¹⁷ But the wisdom which comes down from above is like this:

> It is pure,
> it seeks peace,
> it is gentle,
> it listens to reason,
> it is full of mercy,
> it does good deeds,
> it knows what is right,
> it is sincere.

¹⁸ Those who love peace will sow peace wherever they go. And the harvest they gather will be a very good life.

4 What do you think causes wars? What causes quarrels among you? Is it not the passions which are at war inside yourselves? ² You desire what you do not have and so you kill. You want what others possess and you cannot get it, so you fight or you wage a war.

What is the real reason you do not have what you want? It is because you do not ask God for it. ³ Or perhaps you ask God with a wrong purpose. Perhaps you want things just to use for your own pleasure. Perhaps that is why God does not give them to you. ⁴ Hear me, you creatures who have not been faithful to God. Don't you know that when people become lovers of this world they become enemies of God? When you fall in love with the evil in this world you become God's enemies. ⁵ Do you think our Holy Book is using empty words when it says:

> "When God puts His Spirit in us He is a jealous lover."

⁶ Yes, God pours out His wonderful loving kindness upon us. But we must be humble, for the Holy Writings say:

> "God is against those who are proud,
> but He blesses those who are humble."

⁷ So be humble and do God's will;
    fight the devil and he will fly from you;
⁸ come close to God and He will come close to you;
    you who are sinning, wash your hands clean;
    wash your hearts pure, you whose minds are divided.
⁹ Be sorry and cry for your sins;
    let the tears flow;
    let your laughter turn to sorrow;
    let your joy turn to grief;
¹⁰ humble yourselves before the Lord;
    then He will raise you up.

¹¹ Brothers, never speak evil against one another. The man who speaks evil against his brother speaks evil against the law. And the man who judges his brother is judging the law. If you become a judge of the law you are not obeying the law; you are making yourself a judge higher than the law. ¹² God alone gives the law, and He alone has a right to judge that law. He alone is able to save us or to destroy us. So what right have you to judge your neighbor?

¹³ Listen to me, you who feel so sure of yourselves. I hear you say:

"Tomorrow we will go to this or that town. We will spend a year there and do business and make money."

Why do you talk like that? ¹⁴ You do not know anything about tomorrow. You do not even know that you will be alive tomorrow. Your life is like a cloud. It appears for a little time and then it disappears again. ¹⁵ So you ought to say: "If the Lord is willing, we will be alive and we will do this or that."

¹⁶ But instead of saying that, you are proud and you boast about what you will do. Your boasting is all wrong. ¹⁷ A man sins if he knows what is right but does not do it.

5   You rich men, listen to me.
    Weep and cry out, for sorrow is coming upon you.
  ² Your riches are falling to pieces.

Your clothes are eaten by insects.
³ Your gold and silver have rusted.
They are going to be witnesses against you.
They will burn up your flesh like fire.
You have stored up treasure for your last days.
⁴ You have stolen the wages of the workers who cut your grain.
Now you can hear them crying out against you.
The cries of your workers have reached the Lord of Hosts.
⁵ You spent your days on this earth in high living and pleasures.
You made your hearts fat, while people were killed.
⁶ You condemned and killed good men who did not resist you.

⁷ Now my Christian brothers, be patient until the Lord comes. A farmer waits for the earth to bring forth its precious fruit. He waits in patience for the spring rain and the summer rain. ⁸ You, too, must be patient and stand firm in heart. For the Lord is coming. ⁹ Do not say evil things against one another, so that the Lord will not judge you guilty. I tell you, brothers, our Judge is standing at our doors.

¹⁰ So be patient when you have to suffer. The prophets who spoke in the Lord's name suffered in patience. Take them for your example.

¹¹ "Happy is the man who remains faithful to the end." You have heard how Job remained faithful. And you have seen what the Lord did for Job in the end. For the Lord is very kind and full of mercy.

¹² And above everything else, my brothers, do not take oaths. Do not swear by heaven or by earth or by any other thing. Let your "Yes" be "yes," and your "No" be "no." If you take oaths, God may judge you guilty.

¹³ If any one is in trouble, let him pray. If any one is feeling good, let him sing praises.

¹⁴ If any one is sick, let him call the church elders. Let them pray over him and put oil on him in the Lord's name. ¹⁵ And

if their prayer is offered in faith, it will save the sick man. The Lord will make him well, and will forgive his sins.

[16] Confess your sins to one another. Pray for one another to be healed. The prayer of a man of God has great power. [17] Look at the power of Elijah's prayer. He was a man like us. Yet he prayed hard that it might not rain, and for three years and six months it did not rain. [18] Then he prayed again, and the rain fell out of heaven and the earth brought forth crops once more.

[19] My brothers, if any one of you wanders from the truth, try to bring him back. [20] Whoever saves a bad man from his evil ways covers up many sins and saves a soul from death.

James

PETER'S FIRST LETTER
TO JEWISH CHRISTIANS

From: *Peter, apostle of Jesus Christ*

To: *All of you who have been forced to live in lands far
from your former home*

1 I write to you who are in Pontus, Galatia, Cappadocia, Asia,
and Bithynia.

² God the Father has chosen you and he has his plans for each
one of you. The Holy Spirit has made you holy. Jesus Christ
has washed you clean with His blood. So now you must obey
Him. May God give you more and more of His loving kindness
and peace.

³ I thank God the Father of our Lord Jesus Christ for His
great mercy. It was through His mercy that we were born again
to a new life and a sure hope. We have this hope because Jesus
Christ Himself rose from the dead. ⁴ Now we are heirs of God.
He is holding precious possessions for us in heaven. They will
never fade or spoil, but will last for ever. ⁵ By His power, God
is guarding us who have faith until Christ comes. Christ is coming at the end of this age to save us for His own.

⁶ So you can be full of joy even though you have to suffer
many trials for a little while. ⁷ These trials will test your faith
as gold is tested with fire. Your faith is more precious than
gold, for gold can be destroyed. If you stand firm before every
trial, Jesus Christ will give you praise and honor and glory when
He comes.

⁸ Though you have never seen Jesus in the flesh as I saw Him,
yet you love Him. Though you do not now see Him, yet you

have faith in Him. This is why you feel a joy and a glory beyond words to tell. [9] Already your faith is rewarded, for through your faith, God has saved your souls. [10] Long ago the prophets spoke about the loving kindness which they said God was going to show us. They searched and inquired about how we were to be saved. [11] The Spirit of Christ was working in those prophets. They asked the Spirit who it was that would come to save the world and when He would come. And they told beforehand that it was Christ who would come and suffer death and rise to glory. [12] God told these prophets that they were not talking about their own time. He told them that they were speaking of you, and of our time.

Today your Christian teachers are telling you this same Good News of Christ. The Holy Spirit which God sent from heaven has revealed it to them. We now know things which angels have long wanted to know.

[13] So keep your minds awake and ready for Christ's coming. Keep sober. Put your hope fully in the loving kindnesses which God will give you when Jesus Christ comes. [14] Obey Him as true children of God. Do not obey those low passions which ruled you when you did not know what was right. [15] God, who called you, is holy; therefore you too must be holy in all your conduct. [16] Our Sacred Writings tell us:

"You must be holy, because I am holy."

[17] When you pray to God, you call Him your "Father." But now you are scattered in lands far from your home. In these evil times you must be very careful about your conduct, for fear you may not please God. He judges every man by his deeds, and He does not show special favors to any one.

[18] Once you were living under the laws and customs handed down from your fathers, but these were not able to save you. Christ purchased you from these weak laws. He did not buy you with silver or gold which perish. [19] He bought you with His own

precious blood. He was sacrificed like a lamb without fault or spot.

²⁰ Even before the world was created, God had planned that Christ should make this sacrifice. And now at the end of the ages, Christ has appeared. He came and died and rose for your sakes. ²¹ It is through Christ that you have confidence in God. God raised Christ from the dead and gave Him glory. That is why you have faith in God and hope for eternal life. ²² Because you obeyed Christ, He has made your souls pure. Now you are able to love your brothers sincerely. So love one another with a true love from your hearts. ²³ You have been born again. This new birth did not come from the seed of a man's body, which soon dies. Your second birth came from the living word of God which never dies. ²⁴ You remember that the Holy Writings say:

> "All men are like grass,
> all their glory is like a flower in the grass.
> The grass dries up and its flower falls off,
> ²⁵ but the word of the Lord lasts for ever."

That "Word of God" is the Good News which has been preached to you. Through that Word of God, you are born again.

2 Put out of your minds all envy and all ill will. Be sincere. Never try to deceive any one. Never speak evil against any one. ² As newborn babies are hungry for milk, so be hungry for the pure milk of God's Word. As you drink the milk of His Word your newborn self will grow up and be saved from death. ³ God's little children, when you drink His word, you are tasting the very kindness of the Lord!

⁴ Come to Christ. He is the Corner Stone, the "Living Stone" in God's house. Men refused to accept Christ, but He was chosen by God and was very precious to Him.

⁵ Now let God build you also, like living stones into His house of the Spirit. In His house you will be holy priests and you will

offer sacrifices of the Spirit. God will accept your sacrifices when you offer them through Jesus Christ. ⁶ The Holy Writings say:

"Look, I am laying a stone in Zion.
It is the precious cornerstone which I have chosen.
He who believes in that stone
will never be disappointed."

⁷ Christ is indeed very precious to you who believe in Him. But those who do not believe in Christ will be destroyed. The Holy Writings say:

"The stone which the builders refused to use
has become the head of the corners."

⁸ And:

"He is a stone that will trip men up
and a rock that will make men fall."

They are tripping up because they refuse to obey the Word of God. That is the sad fate of such men.

⁹ But you who believe are the true chosen race of God. You are a royal family, the family of the priests of God. You are a holy nation. You are God's own people. Tell all the world the wonderful things God has done for you. He has called you out of your dark evil life into His glorious light.

¹⁰ Once you were "nobody" and had no country of your own. But you have found Christ and now you are "God's people." Once you had not felt God's mercy, but now He has poured out His mercy upon you.

¹¹ Dear ones, you are strangers in a foreign land. I beg of you, keep away from the passions of the flesh which other people follow, for those passions make war against the soul. ¹² Live good lives among the Gentiles. Many of them will speak against you because you do not follow their vices. But when trouble and suffering come they will see how good and brave you are and then they will praise God.

¹³ Always obey the government officials for the Lord's sake. Obey the Roman emperor, because he is the head of the government. ¹⁴ Obey the governors. The emperor sends governors out of the provinces to punish those who do wrong and to praise those who do right. ¹⁵ God expects you to do right. By doing right you will silence foolish men who make false charges against you. ¹⁶ Because you have become God's servants, you are free men, but you are not free to do wrong. ¹⁷ Honor every man. Love your fellow Christians. Fear God. Honor the emperor.

¹⁸ Servants, be subject to your masters and respect them. Honor them whether they are kind and gentle or rough and cruel. ¹⁹ When a bad master makes you suffer, just remember you are God's children and endure the pain. Then God will praise you. ²⁰ But if you have done wrong and are beaten for it, then of course you will get no praise for being patient. It is when you suffer for doing right and are patient that God praises you.

²¹ Christ said that those whom He calls, will suffer. He suffered for us and He left us His example. He wants us to follow in His steps. ²² Christ never sinned. Nothing false ever came from His lips. ²³ When He was cursed, He did not curse back. When He suffered, He never threatened those who injured Him. He trusted God who is just in judging all. ²⁴ Christ carried our sins in His body upon the cross. He died so that we might die to sin and live right in the sight of God. By His wounds we have been healed. ²⁵ You were wandering like lost sheep. But now you have returned to the Shepherd Who guards your souls.

3   Married women, you must be subject to your husbands. Some of your husbands do not obey the Word of God. Perhaps you may win them without a word if they see how well you behave. ² Let them see how sincere you are in your worship of God and how pure your lives are. ³ Do not let your beauty depend upon ornaments or hair dressing or jewels or fine clothes. ⁴ Let your beauty come from inside, the beauty of a gentle and quiet spirit.

That beauty never grows old. It is very precious in the sight of God. ⁵ The holy women of long ago put their trust in God. That is how they made themselves beautiful. They were subject to their husbands. ⁶ For example, Sarah obeyed Abraham and called him her master. You wives are Sarah's true children if you do right and if you are not afraid to face the worst troubles.

⁷ And you husbands must consider your wives and try to understand them. They are weaker in body than you are, but they are heirs of God's grace and of everlasting life, just as you are. So honor your wives. Then nothing will prevent you from praying with them as you should.

⁸ Finally, be united in spirit, all of you. Be in sympathy with your brothers and love them. Have tender hearts and humble minds. ⁹ Do not pay back evil for evil. If you are cursed, never curse back but bless the man who curses you. God has called you to live this way and He will bless you if you do.

¹⁰ The Holy Writings say:

> "He who would enjoy his life
> and see good days,
> let him keep his tongue from speaking evil
> and his lips from deceiving.
> ¹¹ Let him turn away from evil and do good;
> let him search for peace and follow it.
> ¹² For the eyes of the Lord look with favor on the
> man who does right,
> and God's ears are open to hear the good man's
> prayers.
> But the Lord is against those who do evil."

¹³ Men will not often harm you for being full of zeal to do right. ¹⁴ But if you do suffer for doing right you will get God's blessing for it. So have no fear of any one, and do not worry. ¹⁵ Have a holy love for Christ your Lord, deep down in your hearts. Always be ready to answer any one who asks you to explain why you have hope in Christ. But let your answer be

gentle and full of respect. [16] Keep your conscience clear. Then if any one tells lies about your good Christian conduct, he will soon be put to shame. [17] It is far better to suffer for doing right, if God wills it, than for doing wrong. [18] Christ did not do wrong, but He suffered and died for us, who sinned. He needed to die but once to bring us back to God. His flesh was killed but His spirit was made alive.

[19] After Christ rose from the dead, He went down and preached to the spirits of those who had died and were in prison. [20] Their spirits were in prison because in the days of Noah they had refused to obey God. You remember how God waited in patience for men to repent while Noah was building the ark. But they did not repent. So at last only eight persons were saved from the flood and all the rest died.

[21] Today baptism saves us Christians, as the ark saved Noah's family. Baptism does not mean only the washing of our bodies. Baptism means that we pray to God to wash our consciences clean from all sin, through Christ Who rose from the dead. [22] Christ has gone to heaven and is sitting at the right hand of God. God has put all angels and all authorities and all powers under Him.

4 Christ suffered in the flesh for you, and you must prepare yourselves to suffer also. The man who suffers enough in the flesh for Christ's sake, has stopped sinning. [2] He lives all the rest of his days in this flesh, trying to do God's will, and he is no longer ruled by human passions.

[3] In the past you did as the heathen do. You followed evil sex desires and deeds. You got drunk. You joined in their low dances and wicked feasts. And you worshiped idols. [4] Now the heathen are surprised because you Christians do not join them in their wicked life. That is why they say insulting things to you. [5] But they will some day have to give account to God.

God judges both the living and the dead. [6] That is why Christ went and preached the Good News to the dead also. They had died and their flesh had been condemned like other men. Yet Christ went to them in the prison of death, so that they might live in the spirit as God lives.

⁷ The end of all things is near. Keep sober and in your right mind. Keep praying. ⁸ Above all keep your love for one another warm. Remember the saying:

"Love covers a great number of sins."

⁹ Invite one another to your homes as guests, and show them how glad you are to welcome them.

¹⁰ Each one of you has some kind of talent. Devote it to helping others. In this way God can use you to scatter all kinds of mercies. ¹¹ If you speak, say what God wants you to say. If you serve, do it by God's strength. And give God the praise for everything in the name of Jesus Christ. The glory and the power belong to Him for ever and ever. Amen.

¹² Now dear friends, do not be surprised at the trial which has come to test many of you as with fire. It is not surprising; it is what you might expect. ¹³ Be glad that you can share some of Christ's suffering. When He appears in His glory, you will be filled with joy. ¹⁴ If people speak against you for following Christ, God will bless you. The Spirit of God and His glory will rest on you. ¹⁵ Of course I do not mean that you should suffer for murder or for stealing or for making trouble or for living a bad life! Never do these things. ¹⁶ But when any of you suffer for being a Christian, do not be ashamed. Praise God that you can suffer for the name of Christ.

¹⁷ The time has come for God to judge the world. His judgment will begin with us who belong to His own family; and if He begins with us, what do you think will happen to those who refuse to obey God's Good News? Our Holy Writings say:

¹⁸ "If a good man is hardly saved,
    what will happen to the man
    who sins and refuses to obey God?"

¹⁹ So those of you who are now suffering for doing God's will must keep on doing right. Trust your souls to God who created you, for He is faithful.

5 Now I appeal to the elders. I am a fellow elder with you. I saw Christ suffer. I also saw His glory, and you too some day will see it. ² Take care of God's flock which is in your charge. Do this, not because you feel it is your duty, but because you love to do it. Do it with eager zeal, but do not try to gain something by it for yourselves. ³ Do not try to be masters giving orders to those in your charge. No, lead your flocks by your good example. ⁴ Then when the Great Shepherd comes, you will obtain a crown of glory that will never fade.

⁵ Young men, you must be subject to the elders. All of you must be clothed with a humble spirit, and you must serve one another. For you know the saying:

> "God is against the proud,
> but He gives His grace to the humble."

⁶ So humble yourselves under God's mighty hand, and at the right time He will lift you up. ⁷ Throw all your cares on Him, for He will take care of you.

⁸ Keep sober and on the watch. For your enemy the devil is walking about. He is like a roaring lion which goes about seeking for some one to kill and eat. ⁹ Stand against the devil. Stand firm in your faith. Remember that your Christian brothers all over the world are also suffering for their faith. ¹⁰ You have to endure these sufferings only a little while. God in His great grace, will make you strong and well and perfect so that nothing can pull you down. Through Christ, God has called you to His everlasting glory, ¹¹ where He rules for ever and ever. Amen.

¹² Silvanus has been writing this short letter for me. I have known him as a faithful brother. We have written this short letter to you to encourage you. We are sure that you have the true grace of God. Stand fast in His grace.

¹³ Your sister church here in this "Babylon," sends you her greetings. She has been chosen by God just as you were.

My son Mark sends his greetings.

Give one another a loving kiss for me.

Peace to all of you who are in Christ.

Peter

PETER'S SECOND LETTER

From: *Simon Peter, servant and apostle of Jesus Christ*

To: *You who have the same precious faith that we have. We have this faith because our God and Savior Jesus Christ is perfectly good.*

² May you have more and more of God's grace. May He give you peace. May your knowledge of God and of Jesus our Lord ever increase.

³ He has used His divine power to give us everything we need for leading a good Christian life.

The first thing He gave us was the knowledge of Himself.

He called us. His virtue and His glory drew us to Him.

⁴ Then God gave us His great precious promises.

Through these promises we can escape from the death which follows evil passions.

God also gave us His divine nature.

⁵ Therefore you must have faith;

and besides faith you must try hard to have virtue;

and besides virtue you need to get knowledge;

⁶ and besides knowledge you must have self-control;

and besides having self-control you must stand firm;

and besides standing firm you need to serve God;

⁷ and besides serving God you need to love your brothers;

and besides loving your brothers, you must love everybody.

⁸ As you grow better and better in all these things you will also better understand our Lord Jesus Christ. Your lives will be useful and you will bear much fruit. ⁹ Whoever does not practice these things is like a blind man, or a man who can see only a little way ahead of him. He has forgotten that Christ made him clean from his old sins. ¹⁰ So try hard, brothers, to prove by your good life that God did truly call you and choose you. If you do this you will never fall. ¹¹ And then, when the time comes for you to enter the eternal Kingdom of our Lord and Savior Jesus Christ, you will find a glorious door opening for you.

¹² I intend to keep reminding you of these things again and again, even though you know them and are firm in holding the truth. ¹³ As long as I still live in this body, I think I ought to keep you from forgetting them.

¹⁴ I know I shall soon put off my tent (that is, my body) here on earth. The Lord Jesus Christ has told me I shall not remain much longer. ¹⁵ So I am writing these things down to make sure you will be reminded of them after I am gone.

¹⁶ I have told you about Jesus Christ and His power. I told you He is coming again. This is no clever invention; it is the truth. I myself saw Christ's majesty. ¹⁷ I saw him receive glory and honor from God the Father. I heard the voice which came to Him from the God of Glorious Majesty:

"This is my Son whom I love. With Him I am
well pleased."

¹⁸ We who were there with Christ on the holy mountain, heard that voice out of heaven.

¹⁹ This helps us to have great confidence in the words of the prophets. Pay attention to their words as to a lamp which shines in our dark world. Study the prophets until the new day dawns and the bright morning star rises in your hearts.

²⁰ But you cannot understand what the prophets in our holy books mean unless the Holy Spirit helps you. ²¹ The true

prophets never spoke by their own free will. They were moved by the Holy Spirit and they spoke what God told them to say.

2 There were also false prophets. And today false teachers will come among you. They will try to teach you what is not true. They will try to destroy your faith. They will deny the Master Who bought them on the cross. But they will bring swift ruin upon themselves.

² Many people will follow these false teachers in satisfying their lowest passions. Because of their evil ways, the true Christian life will be given a bad name. ³ Because they want your money, these teachers will try to deceive you with false promises. But they will be destroyed. Long ago God gave His sentence against such evil men.

⁴ God did not even spare the angels when they sinned. He threw them into hell and locked them in dark prisons down below. There they will stay until the day of judgment. ⁵ God did not spare the men of the ancient world when they sinned. He brought a flood upon the world because men were wicked. And God saved only Noah and seven members of his family, because Noah preached right living.

⁶ God also completely destroyed the cities of Sodom and Gomorrah with fire. He made those cities an example to warn wicked men how they, too, will end. ⁷ God saved Lot, that good man who suffered so much at seeing the sex vices of those wicked people. ⁸ What that good man saw and heard of their evil deeds, gave his pure soul great pain day after day.

⁹ The Lord knows how to save good people when they are tempted. He also knows how to punish wicked men until the judgment day. ¹⁰ He punishes especially those who are slaves of low sex habits and who do not obey the will of God.

These evil men are very daring and self-willed. They are not afraid to curse the very angels in heaven. ¹¹ Even the angels, though they have great power, dare not curse anybody before the Lord. [12] But these evil men have no more reason than animals. They are like animals which are born to be caught and killed. They are slaves of their own instincts. They curse things they do not understand. In their evil, they will be destroyed. [13] They will have to suffer for their many evil deeds. In open daylight they commit their low sins with no shame. They are like disease spots and running sores in our society. They eat too much and drink too much, and while they are drunk their talk is loud and foolish. [14] They cannot look at women without wanting to sin with them. They can never sin enough to satisfy themselves. They tempt weak people to join them in doing evil.

They plan in their hearts to take everything they can get from other people. Like children of the devil, they are under a curse. [15] They have wandered from the right road and have taken the wrong road.

They are following the road that the prophet Baalam, the son of Beor, followed for a while. He had his heart set on gaining wealth in wrong ways. [16] For this God condemned him. God made a dumb ass speak to him with a man's voice. The ass prevented him from carrying out his mad purposes. The prophet Baalam repented. [17] But these evil men among you today do not repent. They are like dried up water holes. And their end shall be as the clouds driven by a storm. The deep darkness below the earth is waiting to receive them.

[18] They make loud foolish boasts about their wicked pleasures. They tell low stories about passions of the flesh, and so tempt weak men who are breaking away from vice. [19] They talk about being "free," but they themselves are slaves to sin. For whatever overpowers a man makes him its slave.

[20] Through knowing our Lord and Savior Jesus Christ, you have escaped from the low vices of the world around you. Do not get caught again in those sins. If you do, your last state will be worse than your first. [21] It is better for a man never to know God's right road, than to know it and later turn away from

God's holy commands. ²² Those wicked men prove how true the old saying is:

> "A dog which throws up its food turns back to
> eat it again, and the pig that has just been
> washed returns to roll in the mud."

3 My dear friends, this is the second letter which I have written to you. In both these letters I have urged you to be very straight and honest in your thinking. ² I wanted you to remember what the old prophets said would happen. I wanted you to remember also what our Lord and Savior told you through the mouths of us apostles.

³ You must expect that in the last days many men will follow their own passions and will make sport of our faith. ⁴ They will say:

"You promised us that your Lord would come back. Where is He? Your fathers have died, but things are just the same as they were since the world was created."

⁵ These men refuse to remember the vast reaches of time in which God works. It was ages ago when God first made the world by His word of command. Long ago the dry land came out of the waters and was surrounded by the seas. ⁶ Long after that, God sent the great flood which covered the land so that the wicked died in the waters.

⁷ God is now waiting until the Judgment Day. He says that He will then destroy the heavens and the earth with fire, and the wicked will die.

⁸ Dear friends, we must not ignore this lesson of the ages.

> "To the Lord a day is as a thousand years,
> And to Him a thousand years are as a day."

⁹ Some men say the Lord is slow about keeping His promises. No, God is not slow. But He is very patient, and He is waiting for men to repent, because He does not want any one to be

lost. [10] But the Judgment Day of the Lord will come as quietly as a thief. And on that day the heavens will pass away with a great noise. The elements will be destroyed by fire. The earth and all that men have ever built upon it, will be burned up.

[11] Since the world will end like this, think how holy you ought to be and how you ought to serve God. [12] While you are waiting, you can look with earnest desire for the day of God to come, when the heavens will burn up and elements will be melted with fire. [13] For God has promised us that there will be a new heaven and a new earth where everything and everybody will be good. We are looking forward to that day.

[14] Dear friends, while you wait for His coming, try hard to be at peace with one another. Try hard to be found without a spot or fault when He comes. [15] And remember that the Lord has waited so long in patience in order to give us all a chance to be saved.

Our dear brother Paul also wrote you about this, as God made him wise. [16] He spoke about the coming of the Lord in all his letters. Some things in his letters are hard to understand. Ignorant men who are not firm in their faith, are twisting his letters in a way that will bring those men to ruin. They have twisted the other holy writings in the same way.

[17] Dear friends, I tell you these things before they happen. I want you to be on your guard against the mistakes of men who obey no law. Never let them shake your solid faith.

[18] Keep growing in grace. Grow also in the knowledge of our Lord and Savior Jesus Christ.

To Him be the glory now and through all eternity. Amen.

Peter

JOHN'S FIRST LETTER

My dear Children:

1 Christ existed before time began. Yet many of us have heard His voice. We have seen Him with our own eyes. We have touched Him with our own hands. He brought us the Word of eternal Life. He Himself was that Word of Life. ² The Life appeared as a man upon this earth and we saw Him here. We bear witness to Him. Christ the eternal Life Who had always been with the Father, came and revealed Himself to us. ³ We tell you what we have seen and heard, so that you may share the dear friendship with Him which we have. This friendship of ours is with the Father and with His Son, Jesus Christ. ⁴ We are writing about Him to you because we want you to be full of joy. ⁵ This is the message we heard from Him. We tell it to you,

"God is light. In God there is no darkness at all."

⁶ We may say that we are His dear friends; but if we do evil deeds such as other men do in the dark, we are lying and not living the truth. ⁷ We must walk in the Light, as Christ is in the light. Then we will be dear friends of one another. And the blood of Jesus will make us clean from all sin.

⁸ If we say that we have no sins, we are deceiving ourselves. We are not telling the truth, for we all have sins. ⁹ If we confess our sins, God is good and faithful, and He will forgive us. He will clean out all the sin that is in us. ¹⁰ God says that all men have sinned. So if we say that we have not sinned, we really say that God is not telling the truth. Then God's Word does not rule our lives.

2 My little children, I am writing these things to you so that you may not sin. But if any of you does sin, Jesus Christ, who never sinned Himself, will ask the Father to forgive you. [2] For Jesus Christ gave His life to save us from sin. He died to save not only us but the whole world.

[3] We can be sure that we know Him if we keep His commands. [4] A man who says, "I know Christ," but breaks His commands, is not telling the truth and is not living the truth. [5] If a man obeys Christ's words, his love for God is truly perfect. That love in us is what makes us sure that we are in God. [6] He who says, "I live in Christ," ought to live as Christ lived.

[7] Dear friends, to you this is not a new command that I am now writing. It is the same command as that which Christ gave us at the beginning. It is the same command which you have heard from us before. [8] But to the world it is really a new command. The way Christ loved and the way you love are new in this world. The darkness of hate is passing away, and the true light of Christ's love is beginning to shine.

[9] A man who says he is in the light of Christ's love but hates his brother is not in the light. He is still in the darkness. [10] The man who loves his brother is living in the light. If he walks in that light, he will not fall down. [11] But the man who hates his brother is in the darkness and is walking in the darkness. He does not know where he is going, because he cannot see in the dark.

[12] Little children, I am writing to you because your sins are forgiven for Christ's sake.

[13] Fathers, I am writing to you because you now know the Christ who lived before the world began. Young men, I am writing to you because you have defeated the Evil One. Children, I write to you because you know the Father.

[14] Fathers, I write to you because you know the Christ who lived before the world began. Young men, I write to you because you are strong. The word of God lives in you, and you have defeated the Evil One.

¹⁵ Do not love the ways of the world nor the things of the world. If any one loves the ways of the world, he will not love the Father.

¹⁶ The evil in the world did not come from God. The passions of the flesh, the evil desires of the eyes, and pride of the mind, all come from this evil world. ¹⁷ The world with its passions is passing away. But the man who does the will of God will live for ever.

¹⁸ Children, this is the last hour. You have heard me say that the enemy of Christ will come. He is called the "antichrist." Well, many antichrists have already come. This is why we feel sure that it is the last hour.

¹⁹ Those antichrists have gone away from among us. They never really belonged to us in their hearts. If they had belonged to us, they would have continued with us. But they have left us. It is now plain that none of them ever belonged to us.

²⁰ But all of you have been chosen by the Holy One, and you all know the truth. ²¹ I am writing to you because you know the truth, and not because you do not know it. You can tell the truth from a lie.

²² Who, then, is telling a lie? You know that it is the man who denies that Jesus is the Christ. Any man who denies the Father and the Son is an antichrist. ²³ If a man denies the Son, that man does not love the Father. He who confesses the Son also has the Father.

²⁴ Let what you heard from the beginning, live in your heart. For then you will be living in the Son and in the Father.

²⁵ And if you live in Christ you will have eternal life, for He promised it to us.

²⁶ I have written all this to warn you against those who would like to deceive you.

²⁷ The Holy Spirit which Christ poured upon you still remains in you. You do not need any one else to teach you. The Holy Spirit will teach you everything that you need to know.

The Holy Spirit teaches only the truth. He cannot lie. So live in Christ as the Holy Spirit has taught you to do.

[28] Dear children, live in Christ. Then when He appears, you will receive Him with perfect confidence. You will not hide from Him in shame, when He returns. [29] You know that Christ is perfectly good; you know that every one who lives right is His child.

3 Just think what great love the Father has for us, that He calls us His children. "Children of God," that is what we are! The world does not know us because it does not know our Christ. [2] Dear friends, we are now God's children. We do not yet know what we shall be. But we do know that when Christ appears, we shall see Him as He really is, and so we shall be like Him. [3] Every one who has this hope in Christ lives a pure life, as Christ is pure.

[4] Every one who sins breaks the law. That is what sin is— breaking the law. [5] You know that Christ came to take away our sins, [6] and no one who lives in Christ sins. No one who lives in sin has really seen Him or known Him.

[7] So, dear children, do not let any one deceive you. A man who does right, is good even as Christ Himself is good. [8] A man who continues to live in sin, shows that he is under the control of the devil. For the devil has been sinning from the beginning. The Son of God came to destroy the evil works of the devil.

[9] Any one who is born again and who is a child of God, does not commit sin. God's nature is in Him. He cannot live in sin because he is born again and he is God's child.

[10] I will tell you how you can tell who are the children of God, and who are the children of the devil. If a man does not live right and does not love his brother, you can be sure that he is not God's child. [11] From the very beginning, you heard the message that we must love one another.

[12] We must not be like Cain, that child of the Evil One, who murdered his brother Abel. And why did he murder Abel?

Because his own deeds were wicked, and Abel's deeds were good. [13] Brothers, if the world hates you for doing good, do not be surprised.

[14] We know that we have passed out of death into life, because we love our brothers. He who does not love his brother, remains in death. [15] Any one who hates his brother, commits murder in his heart. You know that any one with murder in his heart, does not have eternal life in him.

[16] In Christ we saw what real love is. We saw it when Christ gave His life for us. We ought also to give our lives for our brothers.

[17] Suppose some one who has this world's goods, sees a brother in need of help. If he refuses to help that brother, God's love does not live in him. [18] Little children, let us love, not just in words and fine speeches. Let us prove that our love is true by doing kind things. [19] Our deeds will then prove that our love is true, and our hearts can feel sure that God is pleased. [20] And when we feel our hearts condemning us, remember that God is wiser than our hearts. He knows everything about us, and in His love He forgives our sins.

[21] When our hearts do not condemn us, dear friends, then we go to God in perfect confidence. [22] He will give us every good thing we desire, because we keep His great commands and do what pleases Him.

[23] These are His commands:

First, believe in His Son Jesus Christ;
Second, love one another as Christ commanded us to do.

[24] All who keep these commands of His are living in Him, and He lives in them. We know that He really lives in us by the Spirit of love which He has given us.

4   Dear friends, do not believe every spirit. You must test the spirit in men to see whether it really came from God. For many false prophets have been traveling over the world. [2] Here is how

to test whether they have God's Spirit. If a man teaches that Jesus was God's Christ living in the flesh, that man speaks for God. ³ But if a man does not confess Jesus, he is not speaking for God. That man has the spirit of the antichrist. I warned you that the spirit of antichrist was coming, and now it is here in the world.

⁴ Little children, you are God's children. You have won a victory over the false spirits. Christ, who is in you, is greater than the devil who is in the world. ⁵ The antichrists are the world's children. What they say comes from the world. That is why the world listens to them. ⁶ We are God's children. Those who know God listen to us. The man who is not God's child will not listen to us. That is how we can tell whether a man has the true spirit or the false.

⁷ Dear friends, let us love one another. Love comes from God. He who loves is born of God and knows God. ⁸ He who does not love, does not know God. For God is love.

⁹ God showed us what real love is, when He sent His only Son into the world so that we might live through Him. ¹⁰ We see what true love is, not in our love for God, but in His love for us. His love was so great that He sent His Son to save us from our sins by dying on the cross. ¹¹ Dear friends, if God loved us that much, we ought to love one another.

¹² No one has ever seen God. But if we love one another, God lives in us. When He lives in us, He makes His love in us perfect. ¹³ He has given us His own Spirit. That is how we are sure that He Himself lives in us and we live in Him.

¹⁴ We saw Jesus Christ, and we bear witness that the Father sent Jesus His Son, to save the world. ¹⁵ If you confess that Jesus is the Son of God, then God lives in you and you live in God.

¹⁶ We know how great God's love is. That is the reason we believe He loves us so much.

God is love. He who lives in love lives in God, and God lives in him. ¹⁷ In this world we are living in love, as He lives. The love in us is so perfect that we can wait without any fear for the judgment day. [18] We are not afraid of God when we love Him. Perfect love drives out all fear. When people fear, it is because they are afraid of punishment. So long as a man is afraid that God will punish him, he shows that his love is not yet perfect.

[19] We must love our brothers because God first loved us. [20] If a man says, "I love God," but hates his brother, that man is lying. For he who does not love his brother whom he can see, certainly does not love God whom he cannot see. [21] Christ gave us this command:

"He who loves God, must love his brother also."

5 All who believe that Jesus is the Christ are God's children. Any one who loves the Father, will also love His children. [2] We know that if we love God and keep His commands, we must love His children, for that is what He commanded. [3] Of course if we love God, we do keep His commands—and they are not hard to keep.

[4] All of us who are born of God are gaining the victory over the world. It is our faith which gives us the victory. [5] Who is winning the victory? Any man who believes that Jesus is the Son of God. That man is winning the victory!

[6] When Jesus Christ came, there were two signs that He was the Son of God. The first sign came on the day when He was baptized with water, and God said, "This is My dear Son." The second was when He shed His blood on the Cross for us. So water is one witness; Christ's blood is a second witness. [7] But there is also a third witness. That is the Holy Spirit, and the Holy Spirit tells the truth. [8] So there are these three witnesses to the fact that Jesus is the Son of God. They are the Holy Spirit, the water, and the blood. These all agree that Jesus is God's Son. [9] In court we accept the evidence of men. The evidence which God gives is far better than that of men. God Himself bore witness that Jesus was His Son. [10] Yes, and any one who

believes in the Son of God has the proof right in his heart. That proof is the Holy Spirit.

But if any one does not believe what God said about Jesus, he really says that God is lying. For he refuses to believe what God said about His Son.

[11] God also bore witness that He is giving us eternal life through His Son. [12] So the man who has the Son, has this eternal life. He who does not have the Son, does not have this eternal life.

[13] I am writing this to you who believe in the Son of God, because I want you to be sure that you do have eternal life. [14] We can have perfect confidence in Christ. We know that if we ask Him for anything that He wants us to have, He listens to us. [15] We know that He hears whatever we ask, so we know that we shall have the things we ask for.

[16] If any one sees his brother committing some sin which has not killed his soul, he should pray for that brother. Then God will put new life in that brother and save him.

There is, however, a kind of sin which kills the soul. I do not say it will do any good to pray for a man whose soul is dead. [17] Any kind of doing wrong is of course a sin. But many sins are not the kind that kill the soul.

[18] We know that a true child of God does not sin, because the Son of God protects him and the Evil One cannot touch him.

[19] We know that we are children of God. But we also know that the world around us is in the power of the Evil One.

[20] We know that the Son of God has come and taught us who the true God is. We are living in the true God and in His Son Jesus Christ. Because we know the true God, we have eternal life.

[21] But, my little children, you must keep away from idols.

John

JOHN'S SECOND LETTER

From: *John the Elder*

To: *The Lady whom God called*

I write to you, dear lady, and to your children. I truly love you all. And all who know the truth love you. ² We love you because God's truth lives in you and in us and will be in us for ever. ³ Because we have God's truth and love, grace and mercy and peace will be with us. These come from God the Father and from Jesus Christ, His Son.

⁴ I was filled with joy when I met some of your children, for I found them obeying the truth just as the Father commanded us to do.

⁵ I beg of you, lady, let us all love one another. This is no new command. Jesus gave it to us at the very beginning. ⁶ The command which you heard from the very beginning was this: "You must live in love." If we follow that command we will love one another.

⁷ Many men have gone out over the world deceiving people. These men do not confess that Jesus was the Christ Who came in the flesh. Such men are antichrists. Many people are being deceived by them. ⁸ Watch yourselves so that you never lose the things that we are working for. Hold on to them and you will win your full reward.

⁹ Any man who does not follow the true teaching about Christ does not have God. He who follows the true teaching about Christ has both the Father and the Son.

¹⁰ So if any one comes to your church and does not teach the truth about Christ, do not receive him into your house. Do not even greet him. ¹¹ For if you do greet him, you are sharing his wicked work.

¹² I have much more to write to you, but I would rather not

put it on paper. I hope to come to you and talk to you face to face. Then our joy will be complete.

¹³ The children of your sister, whom God called, are here with me and they send you their greetings.

John

JOHN'S THIRD LETTER

From: *John the Elder*

To: *My dear friend Gaius, whom I truly love*

² Dear friend, I pray that you may have good success and good health. I know your soul is well.

³ I was full of joy when some of the brothers came back home praising your true Christian life. You are indeed following the truth. ⁴ I could not have greater joy than to know my children follow the truth.

⁵ Dear friend, you proved yourself to be a real Christian when you helped our brothers, especially since they were strangers to you. ⁶ When they got back here, they praised your love before our whole church.

Now they are coming your way again. As they go on their journey, give them your help, as God would have you do. ⁷ For when they started out on this journey for Christ's sake, they refused help from any one except Christians. ⁸ We all ought to support such men. If we support them, we will be their fellow workers in teaching the truth.

⁹ I wrote a letter to the church in your city some time ago. But Diotrephes wants to be the head of the church himself, so he does not recognize my authority to write such letters. ¹⁰ If I come, I want to discuss with you what he is doing, how he is telling evil stories about me. He does not stop with that. He refused to welcome the brothers whom we sent. When some

people in your church wanted to welcome them, he refused to permit it. He even put our brothers out of the church.

¹¹ Dear friend Gaius, we must not imitate evil men. We must imitate good men. He who does good comes from God. He who does evil has not seen God.

¹² Demetrius is being praised by every one. The truth which he preaches is itself praising him. I also add my witness for Demetrius and you know that I tell the truth.

¹³ I have many more things to tell you, but I would rather not write them on paper. ¹⁴ I hope to see you soon. Then we will talk together face to face.

¹⁵ God give you peace. Our friends here wish to be remembered to you. Remember me to every one of our friends there by name.

John

LETTER OF JUDE

From: *Jude*

To: *All who serve Christ*

I am a servant of Jesus Christ and the brother of James. I write to all of you whom God has called. God, the Father, loves you, and Jesus Christ will keep you true.

² May you have more and more of God's mercy and peace and love.

³ Dear friends, I have been eager to write to you about the faith which is able to save us. I urge you to defend our faith which God gave once for all to His people.

⁴ Some wicked men have gotten into our churches by secret means. They neither believe nor obey God. They will be condemned as they deserve. They deserve it because they twist the mercy of God to mean that they can practice sex vice. They deserve it because they deny that Jesus Christ is our Lord and Master.

⁵ I must remind you that God's patience has a limit. This is what you were taught very carefully before. God saved the people of Israel out of Egypt but those who refused to obey Him were later destroyed.

⁶ Even the angels must obey. Some of the angels refused to remain where God had placed them. So they were thrown into chains and are kept in darkness below the earth until the judgment day.

⁷ Sodom and Gomorrah and the cities near them teach us the same lesson. They were foul with evil passions and sex vice. They were destroyed by the eternal fire and now they serve as a warning to us all.

[8] Yet now these false men, who got into our churches with their wicked dreams, make their flesh foul with sin. They refuse to obey the laws of God, and they dare to curse the glorious beings in heaven.

[9] These bad men are bolder than the archangel Michael. When he was disputing with Satan over the body of the dead Moses, the archangel did not dare to curse Satan. All he said to Satan was: "The Lord will rebuke you." [10] But these bad men in our churches are cursing anything they cannot understand. They do not reason, but they follow their instincts like animals. They will be destroyed. [11] Terrible will be their end. They are going the way of Cain.

They think of nothing but making money. That is the same mistake as the prophet Balaam made. They will perish for rebelling against God just as Korah perished. [12] It is a shame to allow these men to be in your love feasts. They get drunk and are loud and rough and have no regard for any one but themselves. They are like clouds which give no rain but are carried along by the wind. They are like dead trees which bear no fruit and are pulled out by the roots in the autumn. [13] They are like the wild waves which throw on the shore the foul smelling things beneath the sea. These bad men are like wandering stars which appear once in the sky, and then sink below the earth in the west never to return.

[14] These are the men whom the prophet Enoch condemned. (He was the seventh man in the family line after Adam.) Enoch said,

> "Look, the Lord is coming
> With thousands and thousands of His holy ones.

> [15] "He will judge the world.
> He will condemn the wicked.
> He will condemn them for their evil deeds;
> and for the curses which these wicked men
> have spoken against Him."

[16] These wicked men are always complaining. They are never contented with anything. They follow their own passions. Their mouths are loud with boasting. They try to deceive people with flattery in order to gain some advantage over them.

[17] But, dear friends, you remember what the apostles of our Lord Jesus Christ said would happen to such men. [18] This is what the apostles told you:

"In the last days there will be men who will make sport of our religion. These men will go where their wicked passions lead them."

[19] It is these men who are causing divisions among Christians. They live like men of the world. The Holy Spirit is not in them.

[20] But you, my dear friends, must keep building yourselves up in your most holy faith. You must pray in the Holy Spirit. [21] Keep God's love in you. Wait in patience for our Lord Jesus Christ in His mercy to give you eternal life. [22] Try to convince those who are troubled with doubts. [23] Try to save them from hell fire. Pity those who are slaves to animal passions, but also fear them. You must hate the very clothing which their flesh made foul.

[24] God is able to keep you from falling. He is able to bring you without sin into His glorious presence with great joy. [25] He is the only God. He has saved us through Jesus Christ our Lord. To our King be glory and might and authority before all time, now and for ever. Amen.

Jude